THREE CORNISH CATS

A.L. Rowse

ILLUSTRATED BY
William Geldart

Weidenfeld and Nicolson
London

Weidenfeld and Nicolson
91 Clapham High Street
London SW4 7TA

Peter, the White Cat of Trenarren
was originally published by
Michael Joseph Ltd in 1974.

The extracts from the poem 'Last Words to
a Dumb Friend' from the *Collected Poems* by
Thomas Hardy are reproduced by kind permission
of the Trustees of the Hardy Estate, Macmillan,
London and Basingstoke and The Macmillan
Company of Canada.

ISBN 0 297 77583 9

Printed in Great Britain by
Butler & Tanner Ltd
Frome and London

'Tommer, the Black Farm-Cat'
is dedicated to Phyllis,
who helped me to save him.

Contents

PART ONE
Peter, the White Cat of Trenarren
I

PART TWO
Chalky Jenkins: A Little Cat Lost
75

PART THREE
Tommer, the Black Farm-Cat
87

Peter, the White Cat of Trenarren

The White Cat of Trenarren

He was a mighty hunter in his youth
At Polmear all day on the mound, on the pounce
For anything moving, rabbit or bird or mouse –
My cat and I grow old together.

After a day's hunting he'd come into the house
Delicate ears stuck all with fleas.
At Trenarren I've heard him sigh with pleasure
After a summer's day in the long-grown leas –
My cat and I grow old together.

When I was a child I played all day,
With only a little cat for companion,
At solitary games of my own invention
Under the table or up in the green bay,
At dressing-up or anything to make believe –
My cat and I grow old together.

When I was a boy I wandered the roads
Up to the downs by gaunt Carn Grey,
Wrapt in a dream at end of day,
All round me the moor, below me the bay –
My cat and I grow old together.

Now we are too often apart, yet
Turning out of Central Park into the Plaza,
Or walking Michigan Avenue against the lake-wind,
I see a little white shade in the shrubbery
Of far-off Trenarren, never far from my mind –
My cat and I grow old together.

When I come home from too much travelling,
Cautiously he comes out of his lair to my call,
Receives me at first with a shy reproach
At long absence to him incomprehensible –
  My cat and I grow old together.

Incapable of much or long resentment,
He scratches at my door to be let out
In early morning in the ash moonlight,
Or red dawn breaking through Mother Bond's spinney –
  My cat and I grow old together.

No more frisking as of old,
Or chasing his shadow over the lawn,
But a dignified old person, tickling
His nose against twig or flower in the border,
Until evening falls and bed-time's in order.
Unable to keep eyes open any longer
He waits for me to carry him upstairs
To nestle all night snug at foot of bed –
  My cat and I grow old together.

Careful of his licked and polished appearance,
Ears like shell-whorls pink and transparent,
White plume waving proudly over the paths,
Against a background of sea and blue hydrangeas –
  My cat and I grow old together.

CHAPTER ONE
Bareppa Background

I have put off writing about him as long as possible, for I know it will upset me – as it still does Beryl and me when we think about him or talk about him too much. For I loved him dearly.

He was the most precious possession I had – and the most snobbish, for he was very well born. He was descended from a famous cat in the Cornwall of that day – I suppose the late Victorian age. That was the white cat that had belonged to the daughters of John Sterling, of whom Carlyle wrote the biography.

John Sterling was a great friend of the Quaker Foxes of Falmouth – he was privately engaged to Caroline Fox the diarist. But the engagement was broken off (this is a secret of the family, which I betray) – understandably, for he had several children by his first wife and was dying of consumption.

Two of the Sterling daughters lived on – mementos ot all that high Victorian culture – in the abrupt gabled villa overlooking lovely Maenporth: at any rate unspoiled in those days, before the people got to work on it.

Their famous cat was the ancestor of all the white cats of Bareppa, that delicious late Georgian stucco house, hidden away behind its walls, at the head of the stream that runs down its little secret valley to Maenporth (in old Cornish maen = stone, porth = beach).

Bareppa was one of a number of pretty white-stuccoed houses built just before and after 1800, by Naval post-captains, or officers of the Falmouth Packet Service, celebrated by Byron, Southey, Beckford and other well-known figures travelling abroad by it.

In my time it had come to a member of the Fox clan, on

her mother's side: Violet Holdsworth, née Hodgkin. Her father was Thomas Hodgkin, who, in spacious Victorian days, could combine making a fortune at banking on Tyneside, with writing *Italy and her Invaders*, in more volumes than Gibbon – in its day Hodgkin's somewhat bowdlerised history was known as 'Gibbon for Schoolgirls'. He must have been a saintly man, as wholly good as he was successful at making money.

A Quaker himself, he married one of the Falmouth Foxes, and Cornwall drew him to herself: he and wife are buried in the secluded Quaker burying-ground there.

His eldest daughter, Violet, totally deaf from childhood, made a remarkable life for herself at Bareppa, with the beautiful garden she created and lovingly tended – how I remember its scents, lemon verbena, viburnum, daphne, syringa, and the aromatic scent of the New Zealand tree-ferns that grew in that sheltered valley, looking up across to Rosemerryn, which often appears in Caroline Fox's Diary: the substantial Georgian farm-house on the slope of the hill, with Caroline's memoried Penjerrick over and beyond the brow.

And staying at Bareppa! – well did it deserve its name of Beau-Repaire. If one slept on the garden side, there were all the sounds and scents of the garden; if on the side of the road going up to Mawnansmith, there was the tinkle of the water from the spring running into the granite basin beneath, making music whenever one awoke to hear it.

Besides the rare plants and flowers – New Zealand gunnera, looking like giant rhubarb, crinodendron with little crimson Japanese-lanterns of flowers, azara with golden stars in spring, South African crinum, amaryllis lilies – the chief feature of Bareppa was the birds.

In place of hearing, Violet had given other senses a fuller development. Touch, for example: the birds would come and perch on the back of her hand – *not* the palm (instinct tells

6

them not to) – and she loved the exquisite sensation of the delicate, feather-weight feet. Sometimes when she went into the garden, she would be 'mobbed' by birds fluttering all round her, with the music (unheard by her) of their wings.

Because of her devotion to birds, the cats had to take a very back place at Bareppa. Literally at the back: they were not allowed indoors. They were out of door cats, born and brought up under the shelter of the tree that stood outside the kitchen-door. Birds had the front.

This was a state of affairs incomprehensible to me, who had loved cats from my childhood days. At Bareppa cats were not loved!

Then why have them? I suppose they served a utilitarian purpose, kept the rats away, or the mice down. At any rate, they were kept out of doors, which surprised me too much even to shock me. I was not encouraged to make their acquaintance. The birds were all in all.

This seemed to me a reversal of the proper order of things.

However, when our beautiful slate-blue Janey died, my benefactress gave me one of the litter of kittens from the white cat at Bareppa.

Cats, being proud creatures, as well as subtle, like to have grand names. I used to know a cat that lived in Magpie Lane off the High Street at Oxford, across from All Souls. He had a proper string of names, most of which I can't remember, but they ended in Wellington Koo – a Chinese celebrity of that day.

A great friend at Oxford, Bruce McFarlane, who had the right views not only about the fifteenth century but about cats, had appropriate but single names for his succession of companions. There was Hodge, after Dr Johnson's cat. Then there was Bogo de Clare, after the medieval pluralist Bruce was investigating at the time – I think he held the rectory of Kilkhampton among many other benefices. Last was Jasper – after Jasper Tudor, Earl of Pembroke, uncle of Henry VII.

7

Cardinal Richelieu gave his cats characteristic names –
Ludovic le Cruel, for instance (Jean Seznec once said to me
he was rather like a Great Cat himself, i.e. a panther, with
his terrific political pounce – not the humble and adorable
domestic species). Then there were Mounard le Fougueux,
Rubis sur l'Ongle, Lucifer, and one called le Ténébreux.

Or there was Baudelaire's cat whose beauty was such that
she was worthy to be immortalised – as she has been:

> *Méline, dont la beauté est telle*
> *Qu'elle est digne d'être immortelle.*

But I am not going to tell the story of the Cardinal's cats,
or Bruce's, or my friend T.S.Eliot's (he has told their stories
in verse).

I am going to write the biography – upsetting as I shall
find it, but I always intended to give him a biography as
well as the great (Sir Walter Ralegh, Sir Richard Grenville
of the Revenge, William Shakespeare, etc.) – of this little
Cornish cat so much beloved, who became as loving as he
was loved and was 'humble of heart', like Christopher
Smart's Jeremiah.

All this is but a prelude to his names, for a cat should have
names to describe and define him, where he came from and
who owned him (or whom he owned, as the case may be).

So – his first name was Peter, almost accidentally: not a
name in our family, but of a Cornish lad in the RAF from
my old school whom I had fallen in with briefly. Peter the
Cat came to mean much more in my life – but that's how
he came by his name.

Then Rowse and Holdsworth, the family he came from
and that with whom he came to live. Similarly the place he
came from and the place to which he became so much
attached: Bareppa and Trenarren, where he is so living a
memory – I still can hardly bear to think of the place without
him.

Anyway, he was properly equipped with a necklace of names to face the life he lived there, leaving so empty a place in my heart:

Peter Rowse Holdsworth Bareppa Trenarren.

CHAPTER TWO

Life at Polmear Mine

When he first came to Polmear, Beryl (who kept house for me) and I were grieving for little Janey, so that we didn't take much notice of the new cat.

Janey was exceedingly beautiful, short grey-blue fur and amber eyes: a tiny kitten when Beryl first brought her home from Pentewan. Dinky as she was – a ball of fluff enclosing a surprisingly loud purr – she was a regular tomboy, high-spirited and full of courage, afraid of nothing.

She was mad on games with me: I have seen her appear at the front door looking round for her companion, spot me in the deck-chair in the corner under the fatsia-tree – and at once, like a bolt, a dash across and up into my lap. She regarded me as a property of hers – never left me in the morning when getting up, accompanied me to the bathroom while shaving, wanted to explore outside the window – on the ground floor – and to be let down into the world of gooseberry and currant-bushes outside.

When she wished to come back she would squeak for me, in tiny kitten-voice, to haul her up. I couldn't reach all the way, so she would stretch up for me to get hold of her by the scruff of the neck and scramble up and in at the window. When I sat down on the WC she would settle comfortably in my lap, as if I were going to sit there for ever.

Then there were games in the hall, in which she and I would play hide-and-seek, she tucked away under the telephone table, though quite visible. I would pretend to look in every other corner of the room, until she couldn't bear it any longer and would give the game away with a squeak: 'Here I am.'

Or there was chasing round the hedge – in Cornwall we

call our earth-and-stone walls 'hedges'. This was a wild fast game, I running after the little creature not much larger than a mouse – so small that she couldn't mount the step at the back, and once ran her nose into it flat-bang. I thought she had stunned herself.

Not a bit of it! The next instant she was off again, heart beating wildly, on the mad chase round the hedge she loved best. She was a perfect playmate.

But so fearless. While I was away in Oxford, curious and exploring as ever, she ate the barley-and-poison mixture put down to deal with the snails and slugs, and died of it.

Beryl kept a picture postcard of Hardwick Hall from me, where I was staying with that great character, Evie Duchess of Devonshire, a proper successor to Bess of Hardwick. It says: 'This is the kind of house to live in – filled with every kind of treasure. Have been thinking of Janey Catkin – she would be quite lost here.'

She was not much bigger than a large mouse, but Beryl told me she was growing into a fine cat when she died.

I am glad I was not there at the time. By the time I came home there was another cat. Not to greet me, a stranger to him. Neither Beryl nor I was enthusiastic about him, nor he about us. He was an out-of-doors cat, three parts grown, no beautiful kitten.

I have sketched in Janey's personality, for it was in such contrast to the little tom-cat to whom we were so unwelcoming.

In my absence Beryl had had to go down to Truro to fetch him home in the bus. He had arrived grandly at the bus-station in a chauffeur-driven car from Bareppa, shut up in a box. He had cried all the way in the bus, making such a caterwaul that Beryl was quite ashamed to own him.

Arriving home, the first thing he did was to run away. He remained away for three days and Beryl wished that he was lost. Somehow he found his way back to the back of the house, where she discovered him crouched under the wringer in the wash-house.

By the time I arrived home he would come in and out of the back door for food; for drink he ignored milk and drank water, which was what he had been used to.

Missing my spirited little playmate, Janey, I wasn't very keen on the stranger. Three parts grown, he was a rather gangling adolescent, with a way of holding his tail on one side which I didn't much like. And he didn't take much notice of us. As soon as he had had his food he was off – down on the disused mine-dump where he spent all his time. We saw little of him.

The rather attractively designed house, with its view of the bay, was built on the site of an old tin-mine, formerly called Polmear, from the little fishing village below, which Charles Rashleigh made into a port, in about 1800, and called Charlestown. (Polmear means the big pool.)

Nothing of the earlier mine remained except the overgrown dump among trees in the field below the house. Across the road had been another mine – Dally's Mine (evidently named after a Captain Dallas) – of which I remember the chimney or 'stack', we called it, as a boy.

This property had had an appallingly ugly house built recently upon it, by one of the china-clay people – the usual middle-class bad taste. It had been called, after some mining settlement in America, where he had been: Soulsbyville.

I resisted the temptation to call its opposite number, the other side of the road, All Soulsbyville, and returned to the old name it properly bore: Polmear Mine.

There I mined away like my forbears, Cornish miners – my father's father had worked in a mine the ruins of which I could see from the house, Appletree, with its workings under the bay – at my historical research, Cornish antiquities and local lore, and came up with several books in the years there, 1940 to 1953.

Meanwhile, the new cat – he hadn't yet even a name – worked away on the mine-dump, among the mice, birds, and there were rabbits then. He was half-wild.

One day I caught him in the kitchen, shut the door so that he couldn't get away – and taught him to drink milk. I had had to teach Janey, she came to us so young, just a nursling. I have a snap Beryl took of that operation – with me blowing my cheeks out and making sopping-up noises and saying how lovely it was – and Janey looking at the saucer and then up at me and then just *looking* at it again.

I was having no nonsense with the new cat: I dipped his nose gently but firmly into a saucer of milk. He emerged, like a young bather on the beach at Porthpean, spluttering, but finding it not bad after all.

His nose was dripping with milk, whiskers twinkling with drops, even eye-lashes, as he shook himself and flurried and flustered and fussed. Just like a boy shaking the sea-water out of eyes and mouth and nose.

But he didn't run away, or even try to, while I held him firmly to it. He recognised that it was meant for his good; he quite liked it. He looked up at me without fear – and from that moment was my cat.

Beryl says that it was after that experience – all flustered and flicking milk drops, shaking head and licking his lips – that he felt that he was accepted and became one of the family. Perhaps it may be regarded as his baptism: it was after that immersion that he was called Peter.

Not long after, his former owner, the old lady of Bareppa, came to Polmear and asked to see him. But he wouldn't see her. He disliked anyone strange, whom he didn't know, and couldn't be got to meet her.

I got hold of him and took him up; but he wouldn't go near her, jumped out of my arms, and managed to hide under the sofa.

I observed his reaction with some satisfaction – a suitable

return for abolishing him and his out of doors. He could by no means be enticed to speak to her.

'However, he loves me,' I said smugly, and that assurance was accepted.

My mother, though not fond of cats, certainly helped to tame him, domesticate him. He had been born in 1951, and these were the last two years of her life. Imprisoned in her chair with arthritis as she was, the little cat would lie across her feet and keep them warm. I used to persuade her to nurse him in her arms, which was what he wanted on sleepy afternoons, after a morning out hunting. He was a great hunter until his old age.

With me his relations became more intimate. Beryl would tell him to go and wake me up. My bedroom was on the ground floor: down he would come, jump up on the bed, mount on my chest and bite me gently on the chin.

I think this was a sign of affection, purring the while, perhaps a sexual gesture, for he was approaching maturity.

I was determined to have him doctored, not to have a rampaging old tom getting into quarrels, having his ears bitten and appearance ruined in fights over the females. The phrase was that he was not going to be allowed straying away after the 'strollopes of Charlestown'.

So one fine day – or malign day, according as you look at it – the vet came to fetch him away. He came back an altered cat, having received a shock that made him frightened ever afterwards of strange men, especially appearing with a box to carry him off in.

Having ruined his prospects of sex-life, I accepted the obligation of being his firm, steadfast friend, would always look after him, keep in touch with his well-being and provide for him, even though so much away from home.

After being neutered he became more domestic, more attached to the house – and gradually became more handsome, with maturity a really beautiful cat.

For one thing, his colour: he became pure milk-white and,

with domestication, kept his coat spotless. As a three parts grown, out-of-doors cat he had not bothered. For another, his tail developed into a splendid plume, held properly straight – sometimes, I used to think, like a Victorian dowager's train. Janey's tail was a tiny affair like a mouse's. Peter, though never a large or heavy cat, grew into the beautiful white Persian which he was by nature.

Also a perfect gentleman: his good breed came out. He had exemplary manners, never once in his life scratched or bit anyone, or stole food. Where Janey was quite irrepressible and fearless, Peter was diffident, timid, frightened of everything. My job was to build up his confidence, never let him down.

He was not a clever cat – unlike Bruce's Bogo, a Siamese, who was capable of a rational deduction, or at least association. Used to sitting in front of an electric fire, once, when it was off, he mewed for Bruce to turn it on. Or there was a great character in the village when I was a boy, called Barney: who knew how to insert his paw into the narrowest neck of a cream-jug, but would always tell, with a peculiar miaow, that he had done it – whether a note of satisfaction or of apology for doing what he knew was naughty.

Peter was incapable of these sophistications. It is true that he led a double life: he remained a hunter, much addicted to out-of-doors, until too old to hunt any more. For the rest, his indoor life was dedicated to affection. He became the 'lovingest' of cats, as his former mistress, the 'old lady', would say. He devoted himself to Beryl and me – no one else.

CHAPTER THREE

Transition to Trenarren

Books drove me out of the charming house at Polmear Mine. With me they accumulate like vermin, or just accumulate. My guest-room was rendered unusable with books under the beds, and on the beds. I took to using the stairs. If you accommodate eight or ten books on a stair, you can practically double the number on each stair – until the stairs become impassable.

I suppose it may be regarded as over-compensation for having been born in a working-class house with no books at all in it. What I now needed was accommodation for ten or twelve thousand.

So, selling my nice little house, I accepted the offer to move to a country-house a mile away, lovely Trenarren, which I had always wanted to live in since I was a schoolboy.

With some twenty rooms it was rather too big for Beryl and me, but not too big for my books. (There are now over twenty thousand. I must reduce.)

Moving was a major operation, and involved some strategic planning. There were the things – furniture, rugs, books – to be directed there from Oxford and co-ordinated with moving house from Polmear, while I was stationed at Trenarren at the receiving end. (At that time I could not drive a car: I had to learn.)

Moving Master Peter turned out the most difficult part of the operation. Having won his confidence and love, I thought it would be an easy matter to put him into a friend's car and take him with me.

Not at all. Have you ever tried to *hold* a cat determined to jump out of your arms? I had him in my arms tight enough and thought I could grasp him tighter. Without fighting or scratching, he wriggled like an eel out of my grasp. After that there was no catching him. No one ever could get him into a car, or go near a car – without first putting him into a box.

So he remained behind for two or three days – straying away down on his favourite dump – until, at the end, Beryl got him into the house, boxed him up and brought him with her in the last car-load.

We had heard such things of cats finding their way for miles back to their old home that we decided to lock him in for the first three days, while furniture was still being moved in and men were about in the house. Accustomed to the silent house of a writer, he couldn't bear to hear their voices and steps. He caterwauled and protested, but we were taking no risks.

At night I brought him up to my bedroom to sleep with me – by then, he knew all about that. But he was disturbed in mind and restless; he could not make it out. He would put paws up to the window-sill and look out on the distasteful scene – the magic valley at Trenarren lying still and lovely in the summer moonlight. He would mew with disgust and apprehension at the unfamiliarity of it.

My bedroom at Polmear had been on the ground floor. Here he could not leap out on to the terrace below, as, it is said, the Carlyles' dog, Nero, threatened to do from the sheer strain of intellectual life at Cheyne Row.

Peter would come back from mewing reproachfully at the Trenarren scene, jump on my bed and begin to purr – after all, he knew the bed and I was in it: so much at any rate was familiar and secure. Cats are extremely conservative: dogs rootless and (probably) radical.

After jumping off once again to see if it could all be true, and seeing that I wasn't disturbed or moving, he settled down to sleep for the night.

On the third day, when the men had all gone and there was quiet in the house, we let him out for the first time into the gravelled back court, wondering whether he would come back again or disappear trying to find his way home to his beloved dump.

He wriggled his way across the unknown, open space, practically on his belly – almost like a victim of agoraphobia, or the philosopher McTaggart of Cambridge, making his way round the Great Court at Trinity with his backside to the wall.

The big, steeply sloping lawn from the terrace down to the immense rounded hump of rhododendrons at the bottom had been left unmown for weeks by my obliging prede-cessors: it was now a thick, waving, unmowable hayfield. (Beryl's brother-in-law eventually razor-scythed it for us, before Jack, who looked after the garden, could put the mower on it.)

Meanwhile, Master Peter entered the forest and, invisible and secure, explored it in every direction. What new dis-coveries, what tracks and trails, what scents of field-mice, rabbits, moles!

At the end of his day, he found his way to me in the down-stairs study and jumped up to settle down with an immense sigh of satisfaction – to tell me what bliss he felt, that the place was heaven.

He had accepted Trenarren. From that moment forward we never had any fear of his trying to find his way back to Polmear. Henceforward his life was here: this was his world.

The place was a paradise for a cat and, on the whole, he kept within its circuit – especially after he walked into danger on the farm outside it and met with a serious accident.

Cats are routineers, and know how to dispose of their time, are self-sufficient – unlike dogs, apt to be such bores waiting about to be taken for walks. Peter soon found a favourite spot, which took the place of his mine-dump. Like that it was a place of vantage – on the slope across from my upper study window (at which I write this memoir, without him).

There he would sit hour after hour, at the corner of the western border by the bamboos, intent upon some mouse-hole or mole's – I never knew which. All I know is that, so long as we had him about the place, we were never plagued by moles (the Cornish word for them is 'wants') upheaving their nasty earth-mounds in the lawn.

There he sat – and whenever I was writing upstairs and would call endearments to him across the lawn, he would sit straight up and preen himself, pleased and proud to be spoken to.

Different areas of the big garden had different attractions for him. Jack would meet him on his rounds, up by the old coach-house and stables. Or over in the tennis-court area – very beautiful and fresh, with its outlook down the valley and out between the two headlands to sea.

I had no difficulty in forming the instant resolution that there would be no tennis at Trenarren, so long as I was there. Though a hard court had been made with a foundation of clinkers, Jack and I would dig a hole and pop in any shrub we wanted a place for. So the place is now green and blue and gold with veronicas, rhododendrons, wygielias, buddlias – anything to fill up and keep away the vulgar shades of tennis-parties. All presided over now by a handsome self-sown beech, of the Trenarren variety with serrated leaf, and a balsam poplar to bring its aromatic dusky smell to the house on the south-west wind.

Here was another prowl-place for Peter, though I didn't often see him there.

Outside, the lawn was his. When he was young and full of spirits, and he was with us by the border, he would suddenly take it into his head to dash across the lawn and straight up a tree.

Once when I was entertaining the dear old Mount Edg-cumbes to lunch and they came out on the terrace, Peter dashed out from his hiding-place thinking it was just Beryl and Jack and me. He was brought up short when he found himself confronting a live Earl and Countess, the wind taken out of his sails.

However, Countess Lil joined the number of great ladies who always asked after him in her letters. There were Christabel Aberconway, and Alison and Elizabeth Johnstone at Trewithen, Mary Nevins and Margaret Swain, Mary Isabel Fry and Winifred Freese in America. Only the other day Cynthia Carew-Pole was asking Beryl for him on the telephone. People find it hard to believe he is with us no longer. At All Souls there were Professor Zaehner, Geoffrey Hudson, Douglas Jay and Rohan Butler always faithful in inquiring for him.

Mostly he kept fairly close to the house unless, when young, hunting at night. Even then I would sometimes hear fearful caterwaulings along the terrace beneath my windows. Was Peter entertaining his friends? The noises didn't sound at all friendly. Was he being persecuted by the wilder farm-cats from next door? Were they fighting or what?

I would throw up a window and shout at them – when they would scamper off the terrace into the shrubbery and quieten down. But what with them and the horrid bird I used to call the deadly night-jar – a kind of hawk that hunts by night, of ferocious ugliness, I believe – the high summer nights were not always peaceful.

Sometimes, when I first came home from Oxford, Peter would bring a present up to the terrace for my breakfast – I always knew from the different, rather richer miaow he made to call my attention. Sometimes a mouse, once or twice a bird.

From the latter he was discouraged – 'O you bad cat'. For mouse, or mole, or rat, 'Good cat'. Cats, of course, have no morals: they don't recognise that the former is a bad action, the latter good. To them – so different from humans – all is fair in love and war.

They certainly lead a double life, one hidden from humans – their own secret night-life.

My friend Arthur Bryant had a cat that profited from *two* homes: going out early one day he caught Sammy on his way back from his alternative establishment, his other club, where he got a second ration of food and milk. But he was a sophisticated town-cat.

Nothing like that about Peter, a country cat born and bred, whose hidden life was the out-of-doors life of hunting natural to the species.

This was particularly strong upon him in the latter hours of the night, or very early morning, when he would wake me up to let him out. He had no compunction in disturbing me – he never disturbed Beryl, the disciplinarian: he knew I was the fool about him, and would do anything for him.

If abroad in the house and not sleeping on my bed with me, he would come and scratch gently at my door to be let out – not mew – and never go round to Beryl's door in the side wing. If outside, he knew which were my bedroom windows to mew up at to come in: he wouldn't dream of going round to disturb Beryl.

This was routine. How he knew, I don't know: I supposed he must have registered from my speaking to him out of my windows.

It was sometimes inconvenient going down on a cold winter's night to let him out. But it had its compensations. It meant that I saw Trenarren at all hours of the night as well as day.

How often, letting Peter out, have I seen the old, creviced column of the great insignis pine – the Trenarren Tree which gives its recognisable stamp to the place, like Matthew Arnold's signal elm – rearing up in strangest ashen colour in the pale moonlight, like some temple-column in stone. (Well, this is what temple-columns derived from in the first place.)

At another time the terrace would be all black and silver in the waning moon; while in the east, filtered through the filigree of bare winter trees, would be the first faint rose-flush of dawn upon the ice-blue sea.

Leaving me, the domestic cat, reverting to nature, would sleuth along some trail up the silvered drive towards the gate.

All right when he was young, but when older Beryl did not approve of his coming out of a warm bed into the cold night air. The instinct was irresistible, and I could never resist his pleading to go out anyway. So, as time went on, and he became more chesty – cats are apt to have chest trouble, to be a bit bronchial – I took him to bed with me less often.

In any case, delightful as it was to have him there to begin with, warm and purring and companionable, I could never get him to content himself with the foot of the bed. He always wanted to get up as near me as possible and, as night wore on, to take up more and more of my narrow single bed. For him I should have got a double.

I believe that all cats, small and big, like to lie *on* those they love. Joy Adamson noted this with the lioness she reared in Africa, who would put a paw across from sleeping with her to see if her husband was all right in his hammock.

Peter would lie right across me. And once and again – though he was far from free with his licks, was distinctly sparing of them, and made quite a fuss of imparting this favour – when an arm had got out over the bed-clothes, he has awakened me with two careful licks along my fingers to show how much he loved me.

In the mornings when Beryl came in to draw the curtains, there he would be snug under the coverlet. 'Come on, Peter,' she would say. No movement – just a dazed loving look.

'Push'n out,' she would say; 'you push'n out.'

But I couldn't do that.

'No, *you* get him out.'

So Beryl would slock (Cornish for entice) him out, and, obedient little cat, he would follow her downstairs.

Then I could get up.

Of course he knew how much I loved him. We used to have a joke, Beryl and I: that he loved her more than he loved me, while I loved him more. I wouldn't have minded this, for after all she looked after and fed him, when I was so much away.

It was just that his attitude to us was different. A good cat who never made trouble, he was more attentive with her. He took her more seriously – she was liable to scold him or reprove him; I hardly ever.

He made a difference in that he would regularly go for a walk around the place with her – she had only to say 'Go for a walk, Peter?' and take up her stick. With me, not: I was to all intents and purposes not a man for all seasons – I was here only in vacations – and a man for indoors.

But he knew that I loved him more and took trouble to amuse him.

Sometimes early in the morning, before getting up, I would take him in the crook of my arm. He would lie there with little head on the pillow beside mine. I would wake myself with a sudden snore; so would he. He would yawn; so would I. Both would blink and open eyes to the day.

I used to think how little a difference the two forms of animal creation. John Wesley thought that the souls of the animals went on with us into the hereafter. If so, good for Holy John. If ours do, into whatever hereafter there may be, why not theirs? We are not better than they; less good, I should say.

I once had an interesting conversation with the vet who looked after Peter, about animals. He said he respected them more than he did humans. I said so did I: why did he? He replied that they made fewer mistakes.

I said that, of course, they had a much narrower strip, much less width of choice, to make mistakes in. Humans were presented with many more challenges, offered an altogether wider target for error.

But that wasn't why I respected animals more: it was because, within their own terms, they were more satisfactory, less bumbling and confused and ugly. Cats, for example, were (a) perfect and (b) comic.

They didn't know the latter, and it doesn't do to laugh at them; they are conscious of their dignity and – though they can smile themselves – they are put out by the human guffaw.

But this isn't why I find them so lovable. That goes back to early childhood, a rather loveless childhood, as with 'Saki', who was so right about everything – including the Germans. (He didn't however invent the penetrating psychological distinction between us who like cats and the French, and those who like dogs and Germans. A few notables – Kipling notably – straddle this fence.)

Saki grew up in the care of a couple of grotesque and cruel aunts – so he devoted his love to 'charming cats who gave all the affection the grown-ups did not know how to show'.

The same was true for me, though my parents did their best (almost) according to their lights. The trouble was that, being working-class, their lights were dim.

We usually had a cat, however, always a female as I remember – I still recall Dee-dee, as I used to call her, from earliest childhood. When I used sometimes to cry, the little cat would put an arm and paw around my head and nurse me, with true maternal instinct – which is more than my mother ever did.

This maternal feeling was, of course, not present in Peter; so I used to nurse *him*.

And amuse him – for which all cats are grateful.

Though they know how to occupy their time very well, there are certain interstices which they are glad to have filled up. Especially towards bed-time, I notice.

At the end of his busy, well laid out day Peter would come into the downstairs study for a little attention.

This was the time for games – not quite so riotous as with Janey, a bit more sedate and gentlemanly.

Peter would take up his station half-way up the staircase, while I would hide underneath it and scratch my fingers – making a mousey noise – between the balusters. He would preen and fume and pounce, put out a paw but *never* put out his claws.

Or I would hide behind a door, making a scrattling noise, and pounce on him cautiously peering round to inquire.

Or there was pussy-cat football, played with crumpled up balls of paper thrown into inaccessible corners, where he would lie on his side to push paws in after the rustling paper. Sometimes he would give the paper-ball a pat, by way of kick and run after it to retrieve. I taught him to retrieve a bit. And I get the impression that animals are grateful for being taught a trick, and proud of showing their accomplishment.

It may be that what they are grateful for is for taking trouble with them and over them.

What excited him most was trailing something moving along the floor, pretending it was a mouse. (It is wonderful that they should know about make-believe, about pretending, about acting in inverted commas. Fancy Huizinga thinking that what distinguished man was his capacity for play: *Homo Ludens*. Cats might indeed be addicts of the philosophy of 'As If'.)

I have an old dressing-gown (in which I was painted years ago in Dublin) with a cord round the waist ending in good-sized tassels. It a little surprised me that Peter never tired of stalking a tassel trailing behind me from that dressing-gown.

Or of the string-game. That took place last thing at night and exhausted both him and me. A long string which he chased round and round the legs of chairs until he got tangled up in it, sometimes quite tied up – biting at it, clawing it, sometimes managing to hold while I tugged quite hard,

25

dragging him this way and that, upside down, back feet kicking, sometimes rhythmically.

This was a furious game, in which I sometimes got scratched accidentally, never intentionally, however concentrated on the game he was.

Then the telephone would ring.

I would say, in a sing-song voice, 'Telephone, Peter' – just to make it all right, so that he shouldn't be frightened. But, indeed, he became familiar with the telephone ring.

The game was over. I put him in my armchair and, by the time the conversation was over, he was fast asleep, tired out by the game.

I rather think now that that was the purpose of the game and fury of the chase: to make him ready for sleep. When I picked him up to take him upstairs, he lay like a log in my arms, sound asleep, not holding on by so much as a toe-nail, as when awake.

If he batted an eyelid, I would say in sing-song he recognised as for him, 'By-lows, Peter, by-lows.' And 'up timber'n hill', as the old Cornish said for upstairs, we would go.

CHAPTER FOUR

Oxford Term-Trenarren Vacation

The fundamental routine of Peter's life, however, was dictated by Oxford term and vacations, when I was usually at home. These made the lean months and the fat months for him, emotionally and dietarily.

How he hated my going away to Oxford – one could see the grey look of misery every time in his eyes, and of course he made me quite miserable. He always seemed to know when the good time was coming to an end, even when I learned to put the suitcases out of sight, or did my packing and got away when he was off somewhere in the garden.

The last night at home was too sad: he always *knew*. And going out at the gate and up the lane to Lobb's Shop, the beauty of the bay was lost on me – my eyes were filled with tears. I was a good way on the road to Oxford before I adjusted myself to the life ahead.

When I arrived, the first thing I did was to telephone home, and Beryl would hold him up to the receiver to hear my voice. In the early days he couldn't quite make it out, and sometimes would look all round the room and the skirtings of the wall to see where I was.

Later, he got used to telephoning. For, when in Oxford, I used to ring up every Monday at six. Beryl and he would be waiting by the phone; when he recognised my voice he would purr loudly all the way to Oxford – I could hear him quite clearly. Then I would speak all the familiar endearments into his listening ear.

The Press somehow got on to my telephoning my cat, and rang me up to know if it was true. I soon discouraged that – I was terrified of people getting to know about him: someone might have spirited him away, and held me up to ransom for any amount, he was so much my most valued possession. So the Press got a very sharp, 'What concern of yours is that?'

At home it took him a couple of days to settle into his new routine. For these first days Beryl used to put an old coat of mine on the chair beside my bed; there he would stay until grieving was over and he took up what I am afraid was his normal life, with me absent – though there was never a day when I didn't think of him, wherever I was. Especially going to sleep – thinking of him helped me to go off to sleep (it still does, years after).

Arrived at Oxford, it would be, 'It was very nice to hear you (and Peter – though I couldn't *hear* him) on the telephone.' I was writing *The Later Churchills*: 'am now dog-tired, and off to bed, with an eiderdown over my head. But no Peter.' Going to bed in Oxford was a cold affair after Cornwall.

Another term, I was having to read 'one of the chapters I wrote at Trenarren to a gathering at New College. I'd rather be alone at T. with P.' Or, after an exhausting lecture-tour of the Southern States, on my return 'I have to traipse all over England. I would rather sit in the study with Peter, thank you very much.'

At another return to All Souls: 'I am pining for Peter. He has been much inquired after here, and I hope you arrange for me to speak to him.' My communications with him were by both telephone and telepathy – to which I later on from America added special little letters for him.

One of my relations I hardly knew was anxious to get me to attend a pretentious wedding: 'Impertinent, I call it; and not at all my idea of pleasure. I'd much rather picnic out on the lawn with Jack and Peter, with you in the offing to look after us.' There was all the family I recognised.

Some professed cat-lovers would ask why I didn't take him with me to Oxford. I would reply, with the young Compton

Mackenzie in *Sinister Street* – 'asking permission of the Domestic Bursar would be like asking permission to keep a crocodile in college'.

But the idea was silly. Peter was an out-of-doors cat – Trenarren was his home: he'd have been miserable in Oxford, and I was always having to be away, increasingly in America.

In any case, one could never have got him into a car – unlike poor little Chalky Jenkins from the village below, who was probably thus spirited away. This was something of a safeguard: Peter was so shy of strangers that nobody whom he didn't already know could get near him. With his acute hearing, he could hear the big gate into the drive being opened from far away in the kitchen, where he would growl, 'Gr-r-r', and let Beryl know.

So I had to accept the fact that there was a separable spite that divided our lives, though our undivided loves were one. I had to earn the family living, including his, at Oxford and elsewhere.

I could not afford Arthur Bryant's line about his dog, Jimmy, whom I never loved in spite of his being Cornish. (He was a terrier and, though I like other dogs, especially labradors and spaniels, I do not like terriers.) Arthur wouldn't go abroad, or couldn't go here or there, 'because Jimmy wouldn't like it. Dear little dog', etc.

It is surprising how sentimental people can be about their dogs. Not about cats, of course.

So Peter's normal routine was divided between the big house, where Beryl lived by day, cooked and fed him, etc., and Myrtle Cottage, in the little hamlet below – I can see the roof from the upstairs windows – where she spent the evenings and slept at night. (The big house is too haunted by ghosts – at any rate too atmospherical. I wouldn't sleep here by myself any more than Beryl would.)

Sometimes, if she were unwell, he would find his way down the road to the cottage to visit her. I was always a bit

concerned about his going down the narrow lane – 'imprac-
ticable for motorists', the notice says, but still they whizz
down or up it.

Once, when she had mumps, he came and stayed with her
the whole time, sitting in the window. One of my letters she
kept says, 'Sorry you have the mumps, but glad you have
Peter for company.'

She wasn't so fond of him in earlier years as she became
later, and letters say, 'Why don't you take Peter down with
you if you are lonely? I find him lovely company.'

Of course, a cat is a perfect writer's companion – one
reason why so many writers have been so fond of them. Even
the French, who are apt to be unsentimental about animals.
Or perhaps especially the French, when one thinks how
many of their writers have loved cats, and what wonderful
things they have written about them. And they are often
the writers who speak specially to me.

Colette, for instance – I adore her: though popular, she
is really a writer's writer, properly appreciated (as she was
by Gide, Proust, etc.). She has written about cats with a
sophisticated understanding of the subtlety and rarity of
their nature, the variety in character and personality – which
Richelieu so well appreciated too.

It is a masterly novel that she wrote, with a cat for heroine,
La Chatte: an emotional triangle of a young man, his bitch
of a wife, who is jealous of the cat that loves him and tries
to kill her. That scene is one of the most exciting in modern
fiction. And how original, compared with the vulgarity of
the usual 'triangle'.

The greatest of modern French poets, Baudelaire, wrote
the most exquisite poems about them:

> *Les amoureux fervents et les savants austères*
> *Aiment également dans leur mûre saison*
> *Les chats puissants et doux, orgueil de la maison,*
> *Qui comme eux sont frileux et comme eux sédentaires.*

I don't know about the 'amoureux fervents', but as one of the 'savants austères' the poem speaks for me; and Peter was certainly the pride of the house.

Or there is Barvey d'Aurevilly, who has a particular attraction for me, or Mallarmé, who has the most imaginative tribute to the mystery of cats. (But he was a Symbolist, who saw mystery in everything. No mystical nonsense about Peter: he was simple and humble, diffident and loving.)

Even Victor Hugo and Sainte-Beuve both loved cats: they had that in common, as well as Victor Hugo's wife.

Similarly with English writers. Those who liked cats are often those who appeal particularly to me. I have long known Matthew Arnold's Atossa, and her jumping on his desk to interfere with his writing. (Peter used to do this when young, fascinated by the movements of the pen, when he would put out a delicate paw, so gently, to touch it. I have a snap of him somewhere, sitting smugly on my manuscripts, holding up the work, looking down very pleased on the scene.) Arnold's cat made one demonstration of affection in the morning, then no more all day. Very odd.

Samuel Butler and Miss Savage had that in common, if not so much as she would have liked. The crusty, but fascinating, old bachelor had a cat called Prince, when he lived in Barnard's Inn. A little girl visitor made a great discovery when playing with him (the cat): 'Oh, it's got pins in its toes.'

Poor Miss Savage did all in all to make up to Butler through his cat:

Archly, 'I have christened your cat "Purdoe", a good name for a cat. I baptized it with ink.'

Propitiatingly, 'I hope your dear cat is well. Tybalt, prince of cats, daily gives fresh proofs of intelligence that are truly amazing.'

I have had that to put up with too – unattached females trying to get at me through Peter, telephoning to ask me how he was, etc. – as if he were any concern of theirs, as if they cared tuppence about him, as if I didn't care infinitely more for him than for them. Such stupidity only made me cross – *he* wouldn't be capable of such a *bêtise*: too much tact, a finer intuitive sense than any human.

There *is* a genuine mystery about cats: how much extra-sensory perception have they?

We know that dogs have more capacity for reasoning, or association, as they have a larger cortex. Pavlov (the brute) found that a decorticated dog falls heavily with no control over its limbs. Whereas a decorticated cat falls with its neuro-muscular movement still in control. That is, it has less dependence on the brain.

By the same token, the cat may well have subliminal intuitions that connect it with the object of its love, or other objects. We know that there are very curious phenomena about dogs – of a favourite dog drooping and dying when its master, 'unknown' to it, has been killed away at the front in the war. No reason to doubt the authenticity of such stories.

I do not ever remember such a story of a cat – though, when Bruce McFarlane died, Jasper ran away. There is no reason to suppose that cats – being less dependent on 'reason' – should not have some intuitional sense we cannot explore. Peter knew when I was coming home – no doubt there were indications: the house being prepared, my bedroom made ready. Beryl or Mrs Johns, who loved and understood cats, used to tell him. But, anyway, he always *knew*.

So I used to assume that he would be thinking about me when I was away, or abroad – as I certainly was thinking about him – and perhaps was aware, in some manner we are unaware of, how I was, well or not. (Beryl kept letters from wherever I was, inquiring for him, sending money for his keep, for the tins of meat he preferred, for milk or fish.) Though so much away, hardly ever a day went by without thinking of him.

And certainly the remembrance of me never wore away in his mind so long as he lived.

I shall never forget my first return to Trenarren after a whole winter at the Huntington Library and being more than six months away from home. One would have thought he might have forgotten.

When I came in at the gate, longing to see him, there he was a good way down the lawn playing with Beryl and Jack and someone else. When he heard my voice calling to him, he left the group like a shot, bolted up the lawn and into my arms.

He didn't purr – it might have been thought a reproach for being away so long – he was numbed and cold. I was touched to tears by it and seeing him again. By the time I took him off to bed that night, all was well. *He* was happy, even if I could not explain why I had to be away.

Again there was a fairly regular routine on my return. It was only occasionally that I took him to bed; so in the mornings, for the first three or four days, he would be sitting at the foot of the staircase, rocking himself to and fro with pleasure – in the way cats have, poised more on one foot then on the other.

I would seize him from behind, arm right round his neck so that there was only his white head showing – small, and delicate – cover him with kisses, ending up nose to nose like two Polynesians greeting. Cats have the most sensitive noses; he would recognise this for a very special greeting, and stagger away drunk with affection, purring like a machine.

I brought him to bad habits, I suppose, in feeding him at table; but this was only when I was alone – he didn't appear much when there were people about, still less pester folk at table in the way some people's dogs will. And Peter would only pester me – as with being let out or into the house: he knew (as reviewers do not) how amenable I am, and for him could be got to do anything.

There were limits of course. Once, when he was clawing

33

my knee with such pleasurable expectation that it hurt, I gave him a whack. (He was never whacked: he didn't need to be, he was so well-behaved, never stole, etc.) This was so unwonted and regarded with such disgust that he went and sat in the dining-room doorway, turning his back on me: I was sent to Coventry.

A far more usual scene would be to see me picking out the pieces of meat from my Cornish pasty (well-made and tasty, full of meat, the pastry light and crumbly – unlike the specimens that disgrace the name in London cafés) and ranging them round my plate to cool; piping hot, I would blow on them to cool the bits. Though as keen on pasty as I was, and more anxious for the feast to begin, he seemed to understand all the puffing and blowing was for his benefit. He knew that I would never cheat him, but feed him first before I began. So he would wait more patiently, with an occasional paw on my leg to remind me.

Passing by the door, or peeping in, Beryl would find this a comic spectacle with me blowing to cool his food. ('If only I could write a book!' she would say.) Peter found it understandable, or at least acceptable. And, of course, all cats love to be fed by hand by those they love – they recognise it for the special attention it is. More usually, when the dish was something sloppy, stew or roast, he had his plate set down beside me.

As for me, I was happy with his company at meals as at all times. (Not so with people – what a blessing cats can't talk: one doesn't have to put up with the platitudes, the clichés, the ineffabilities, that fall from the faces of humans.)

Though he knew few words, the word 'Dinner' was one; 'Beryl' was another. Sometimes at night, when he was out ranging round the grounds, I would go and call for him. He usually answered and came. Picking him up, I would say insistently, 'Din-din-dinner ... Beryl, Beryl. Dinner, dinner, dinner.'

This excited his interest: he would get quite restless; and

arrived at the front door would jump down and hurry along the hall into the kitchen ahead of me.

Then there was tea in the study. I never knew whether to call this 'tea' or 'dinner' for him; but usually called, 'Tea, tea, tea', or 'Milk', or 'Milkie Dinkie'.

Anyway, he knew this routine. A saucer of milk before I poured out my tea. For him, biscuits or cake – he had a decadent taste for sponge-cake, and loved biscuits, and brittle shortcake. After this, there would be a few crumbs left over, which he was very good in trying to pick up when pointed out to him – not so good at spotting for himself. (Is this something to do with the focusing of their eyes?)

These were special attentions, special occasions with me: his regular meals were in the kitchen, where he had his own plate and saucer – though he often left the milk, preferring water.

Sometimes, on a hot summer day, when he was comfortably nestled in a shady place on the border where I was weeding, I would surprise him asleep with a saucer of cool, glistening water under his nose, which he didn't even have to move to drink. The look of surprise, then gratification, was its own amusing reward.

The most special of attentions, and somewhat difficult to manage, was when I was having morning tea in bed. Used to being treated equally, he would expect to share with me and look expectantly at the tea and milk being poured out. So I would have to manage a little milk in my saucer, so that he could have his morning tea too.

The rule was never to leave him out, always to share in what I was having. (Beryl had no such compunction, nothing like so soft with him. '*He* can do anything he likes.' 'Whatever Peter does is all right.' 'He can always get around *you*,' etc. Well, of course, he could: I loved him. And, besides he was such a good little cat. 'He doesn't ask for much', said Mrs Johns, sagely. Unlike people again.)

When I was away, Jack would bring him scraps – he was

35

the third figure in Peter's family, a familiar to him, so that
he would come to his call. No one else: only the three of us.
And he knew Jack's name, for I would regularly use it. He
had no name for me – though I would call myself by my
first name in talking to him: otherwise unused, it was only
for him, in the endearments that passed, the nonsense-
language I talked to him.

As Anatole France observed, talking nonsense is a sure
sign of love. It was also like the 'little language' that Swift
talked to Stella – like that, I suppose, a release from tensions.
Certainly, unknown or known to himself, Peter performed
that office for me, was a great help in his turn – just as thinking about him helps me off to sleep still.

I can't go into all the nonsense-talk I talked to him, all
the endearments. 'He is my wow-wow', or 'He is my kwow-
quow', often tongue-twisters beginning with kw, or qu,
rather difficult to say. I have forgotten many of the terms
he used to inspire, still more their origins.

Among verbal endearments there was one that I named
the 'amatory past', in which he was addressed in the past
tense out of love: e.g. 'he *was* my goo-goo'; 'he *was* my
beautifuls', in the plural. There was also the amatory future
tense, rather declamatory: 'he *shall* be my cot', etc., when
he already was. He was also my baw-baw, my quowtie, my
pooket-cattums, or simply 'my boy'. Sometimes he was my
'foo-foo dog-dog'. I think this came from the Chinese bronze
fo-dog I have for a door-stopper. Earlier, I have placed this
beside him when asleep: he would open eyes wide with surprise, but never more. He knew it was a joke, and was not
taken in. Nor even by a toy mouse.

All these terms of address were received with some satisfaction and complacency. Once, when we had a duck in the
larder, and I inquired where was my duck, Beryl affected
not to know which I was referring to. Such games we played
around and with Peter.

The name Wow-Wow came from the kitchen-cat we had

at Polmear Mine before Janey. Not very interesting, she was
too much taken up with her sex-life and kittening: a
nuisance. As a kitten she was nice enough: I used to make
a nest for her in the middle of a woollen rug, where she was
a pretty little companion, black and white long haired, evidently a strain of Persian in her make-up. Then the bore-
dom of sex began and, like Lewis Carroll, I found her less
interesting.

Only one endearment of hers I remember, for it was peculiar, unique. Actually, like the Trinity, it was three-in-one.
She was sunning herself on a summer's day on top of the
wide earth-hedge, on a level with my head. She leant forward
and tweaked my nose, a gentle love-bite; then proceeded to
the lobe of my ear, another little bite; then a strand of hair
on my forehead – she didn't like the texture or taste, and
soon dropped it.

A regular habit she had was to come into the hall from
outside, and let out a loud 'Wow-Wow'. I couldn't make out
what she wanted, for, as soon as I answered, off she went
again, apparently content. I now suppose that this was
maternal instinct again: she simply wanted to know if I was
there and all right.

From these loud 'Wow-wow's she got her name: she had
no other.

Naturally there was nothing maternal about Peter, and
– thank goodness – he knew nothing about a sex-life. I rather
think the female-cats from the farm used to persecute him
for being so unresponsive (in that like his master).

I used to think that if I didn't talk so much nonsense to
him – 'my dee lil' poo', etc., like Swift's 'Nite, nite, MD, MD'
calling himself Presto – Peter might have been a more edu-
cated cat: I might have taught him more words, more
objects, and taught him tricks. He was quite pleased with
himself over the simple trick of jumping over my hands.

He rather liked my singing to him as I rocked him to and
fro in my arms. Bruce's cats seemed to like being swung right

round – this seemed to me too rough, but they had been used to it from kittens. Peter hated music – couldn't bear the piano, especially noisy Beethoven – and didn't think it a joke when I walked him over the keyboard. He hated the wireless, too, though he didn't mind the telephone.

I fear he was not as intelligent as Cyril Falls's cat, who was sitting peaceably on the sofa, when out of the wireless there came, 'You naughty cat!' – and off he jumped at once.

Peter understood endearments better, and loved to be told that he was bew-ew-tiful.

As a matter of fact, all animals love to be told that they are bew-ew-tiful. Whether it is in the tone of voice, or the *ew* sound, they find it irresistible. Try it on dogs – they often find it sexually exciting, and regard it as an invitation to board one. It even works with strange dogs barking away when one approaches their house: they know it is a compliment.

One day at the gate at Trenarren there was a large bulldog struggling up the hill, waddling out of breath, lolloping, tongue hanging out, slobbering. I told him he was bew-ew-tiful (like Ralegh's *Large and Bewtifull Empire of Guiana*) – he came to me at once, eyes dripping with gratitude and sentiment.

He was, of course, as ugly as a gargoyle. But I didn't tell him that – I wouldn't dream of hurting an animal's feelings. (Humans can fend for themselves and, anyway, richly deserve what they ask for.)

His owner said, 'I don't think beauty is the word for it.'

I said, 'But he has his own sort of beauty,' and shut the big black gate.

Sometimes I called Peter the most bewtiful cat in Trenarren – but really there wasn't any competition. I think I must have got that idea from the old person at Callington who was shown Isaac Foot's library. Isaac had some 80,000 books stowed away in the rooms and attics of his sizable house, Pencrebar. When some local tom-noddy was shown over the house, he said 'This must be the biggest library' – words failed him, 'why, the biggest library in Callin'ton.'

Peter was certainly the most beautiful cat in Trenarren – I sometimes amended it to 'in St Austell'.

But why was he addressed as 'my little Teddy Beard'?

This had a more complicated origin, a fusion of two ideas. From infancy to the early years of marriage, John Betjeman took his teddy-bear to bed with him. (I early grew out of this infantile habit.) Once, when Penelope threw the teddy bear out of the bedroom window, there was nearly a divorce or at least – with that devout High Church couple – separation *a mensa et thoro*.

But also an old flame of mine as a schoolboy, for whom I wrote a waltz (I remember it still and how it went: it was in my favourite key, then, of C minor), had a boy-friend called Beard. I was never her favourite. But this is how Peter, by conflation, became 'my little Teddy Beard'.

I cannot remember now all the names he was addressed by at different times, all of them loving, as befits a 'little language'. Norman Scarfe, who knew him well early on, knew him as Peter-nose. I think this was short for Peter-nosegoose, which came from Paul Gallico's *The Snow Goose*.

Endearments? What kind of endearments did he like?

Nothing rough, like Bruce's cats: Peter was rather a pansy, marked by diffidence and shyness.

In any case, the art with a cat is to go gently to begin with, to stroke them less than they would like, so that they make the running, make up to one. The initial gentleness tells them that here is someone who knows about cats.

His ears were very beautiful transparent shells, with the elegant little tufts proper to his breed. Between his ears there were very delicately patterned furrows in the fur. He never minded how many kisses I planted on his forehead, remaining patient while I held his head. He had such confidence that he would run his muzzle into the hollow of my hand,

39

leaving only my end fingers free to flick his ears. He liked that somewhat odd endearment.

Less keen on having his belly tickled while he lay upside down on the gravel. It must have really tickled him and made him kick out with back legs, full force.

The best photograph I have of him is in something like this position – I came round the corner and snapped him on his back sunning himself, the fur on his belly curly and glistening like pale honey in sunlight.

It was always difficult to get a good photograph of him – he recognised the camera and its eye looking at him and then the click: he hated it.

In fact I bought a camera simply in order to photograph him. 'Please may I have a small camera to take the cat?' The shopkeeper looked at me as if I were dotty; no sense of humour, no sense of inverted commas in what I said. (*They*, ordinary humans, can never hear them – especially critics, who cannot tell when a Celt is putting on an act, secretly laughing at them.)

He looked slightly put out, as if I were laughing at him, or down-grading his stock in trade. Actually the cat was a great deal more photogenic than the cameraman.

But, alas, almost impossible to catch. I have a number of him turning away in disgust, when I have come out with camera behind my back hoping to get him unawares; others with him struggling to get out of my arms when someone else was trying to snap him for me. I have a few distant snaps of him by a border sniffing the flowers, or just tickling his nose at them; or coiled up in a garden nest amid pampas or long grass, asleep. Hardly a single photograph that is satisfactory or revealing of his beauty. There is only my memory of him in all his endearing moods.

I suppose he was loved into being the very special – and extremely loving – cat he became, from the rather nondescript waif, almost a stray, he was at first.

He was aware of his beauty – as animals, particularly

horses, are – when fully grown and still in the flourish of his youth. He sported a splendid plume of a tail. Once, when I had a lunch-party, though he was usually shy and kept aloof, he marched into the library to display himself all round the circle of guests, and then, courage failing, sought to go out at the big Venetian window.

'Out?' – this was one of the words he knew. I threw up the bottom of the window and out he leaped, relieved after this unwonted piece of exhibitionism. He never repeated it.

What he liked best in the way of endearments was, at the end of the day, to lie upside down in my lap, coiled round for me to stroke and nuzzle and gently pull the fur of his belly. This was ecstasy: something he couldn't do very well for himself – though cats are self-regarding animals. This gave extreme pleasure: I have known him turn his head with the swiftness of an automaton, holding my hand with paws while I kneaded and rubbed and gently pulled. The purring machine roared. This was bliss.

Another endearment he liked was fluffing out the fur on his cheeks, not playing with his whiskers – that was regarded as an indignity. He liked, too, patting or drumming with my fingers on his nose – again something he couldn't very well do for himself.

Not quite such bliss was lying full length on his back in bed while I went slowly down the surpliced choirboy front, from chin held up for me to stroke throat and then gradually down, slowly, slowly, over knees that kicked with reflex action, down to feet that flicked apprehensively, as if they might be caught in a trap.

I never played any trick or made an unexpected move to undermine his confidence.

And though so nervous a cat, I was touched to learn, in the early days at Trenarren, how complete his confidence was. He got stuck one day up a tree, not very far up, but he couldn't see an obvious way down. I noticed with some apprehension that he was preparing to jump down on me

– perhaps tearing my woollen sweater in the process. So I reached up and fetched him down instead.

I still have mementoes of him, little marks of his claws on the arms and lapels of coats where I used to hold him – it gives me a few moments' sadness to notice his traces long after he has vanished.

I write these words at night at Trenarren, my bedroom window right up to hear the murmur of the summer sea, the leaves of the magnolia looking in to the lighted room; the dark mass of beeches beyond, and one star bright over the bay brimming with moonlight – just like the summer night twenty years ago, when he stood up to the window-sill to look out on the strange scene that would become his home.

No Peter there tonight – or ever will be, ever again. O the strange irreversibility of time, the irrevocableness, the mystery of it all! The window is open on the gathering dark, empty of that dear white presence, and I am twenty years older, nearing my end.

CHAPTER FIVE

Accident and Sickness

He was hardly ever scolded by me, for he never did anything that was reprehensible in my eyes. (Beryl was made of sterner stuff.) There was one exception. I have in the library a beautiful Louis XVI tapestry sofa – with panel of animal design by Oudry. Naturally no one is invited to sit on this precious piece of furniture.

But Peter took a fancy to it, in the curious way cats have of taking to different places for their pleasure. I would find him coiled up comfortably on the tapestry seat, looking up on my approach for the usual approbation. He did not get it.

Another fancied spot was the wide stool covered with malachite-green velvet – for which little claws opening and closing with pleasure, were not good. I had to shoo him off several times – and he was not pleased, could not understand my objection.

He was, however, allowed on the Louis Philippe tapestry chairs – less valuable: poor little fellow couldn't distinguish between Louis Philippe and Louis Seize. So much in human behaviour must remain out of range, incomprehensible and possibly irrational to cats.

He did, however, appreciate the pussy-cat voice in which I talked to him, recognised that that was meant for him. And I think particularly liked being whispered to – no doubt that that was for him alone. He would respond with that gentle sizzling noise, not quite a purr, like a kettle singing on the hob. Perhaps it was his form of singing to me – it was certainly very soothing and welcome.

He hadn't much experience of dogs, since they were not allowed inside the grounds, scratching up the lawn, leaving scuffling footmarks on gravel, treading down flowers in the border. He must have known dear old Rover down at the farm, and his unfriendly successor Spot.

But once Peter was chased inside his own grounds – a great offence to dignity, most humiliating. And by a beautiful and friendly labrador, Apollo, belonging to my friends, the Hartleys. I was horrified and alarmed when I saw the big yellow dog gaining upon the little cat – and shouted furiously out of the window to get the bloody dog under control.

Harold replied peaceably that Apollo had only chased Peter because the cat ran away. And that the dog wouldn't know what to do with him if he caught him. I dare say. But instinct might tell him. And if he killed my Peter I could never speak to them again, etc.

When I came to know Apollo I found that he had an angelic disposition and that it was unlikely he would ever hurt a cat. But I was taking no risks.

Later that evening I went out to look for Peter, who had taken refuge in a remote part of the garden and wouldn't come in. He was sitting in a secluded patch, still swearing at the indignity of being chased in his own property and, when I approached, even raised his paw at me, for the only time in his life.

It was pure pretence, of course, and I was having no nonsense. I picked him up still saying gr-r-, and gave him little smacks, saying 'Beryl', as if coming from the Boss, to behave himself.

That night he slept like a log for the whole night beside me, never making a movement, worn out with the excitement, apprehension and indignation.

While I was away in Oxford one summer term a really serious accident befell him.

In those days there were plenty of rabbits at Trenarren; today only one dinky, kittenish specimen has found its way there, heaven knows how (one rabbit, plus one squirrel, two green woodpeckers, a resplendent family of pheasants).

At Magdalen Bruce's cat had the Grove (where I have seen *A Midsummer Night's Dream* ending in the moonlight) to disport himself in; and the Master had the regular job of defleaing. I followed in his footsteps with the hunter at Trenarren. Fortunately animals' fleas are a different – and cleaner – variety than humans'. Peter would sit patiently while I went through his ears and head, myself saying Grr to express disapprobation, while he gave an occasional squeak of protest. However, he seemed to know that I was bent on his good, recognised the necessity of the operation, and never once attempted escape. He was an exceptionally docile, obedient cat.

One day he came back to the house with a foot more than half off: he had been caught in a rabbit-trap on the farm. Beryl's explanation was that the farm-boy (a pretty primitive type, handsome as Apollo, later drowned on the beach below) must have released the cat, to let him find his way home, where he arrived in a fainting condition.

Beryl laid him down on a rug in my study, gave him some warm milk, and summoned the vet, who put the fore-leg in a splint.

By the time I arrived home, Peter had recovered and was stumping about the house like a man with a crutch, and making almost as much noise. One could hear his approach, his movements about the house like another inhabitant.

Of course, he was a third inhabitant. When I called him a dear little thing (doo lil fing, in pussy-cat language) I used to correct myself: 'he's not a thing, but a person'. And when the form for the Register of Voters came – which one had to fill up under some penalty, which I much resented, never having wasted a minute of my time on voting since the decisive date 1945 – I had the greatest difficulty in resisting the temptation to add to

A.L.Rowse – householder
B.L.Cloke – housekeeper

the name

Peter Rowse – housemate.

After all, I would say, he knew as much about the issues at stake as the electorate.

It was some weeks before we called in the vet to take off Peter's splint. I found I couldn't do it. We used to sit at night in my armchair, he trying to gnaw at the tough linen bandage, while I tried to scissor it off. Both of us were defeated – but, again, he recognised instinctively, as always, that I was trying to help and never made the least trouble.

The great day came when the vet was summoned, the splint removed, and Master Peter was able to leap about, a young cat active as ever.

The dreadful day came when Beryl went away for a holiday, and he had to go to the vet's for his. This became a regular summer routine – and how he hated it!

I was never here to see him go off, of course, and I longed to be the one to go into the town and bring him joyfully back.

Beryl told me he always cried all the way, uttering a loud wail at the gate, '*Ma*', just like a child.

But once at the vet's he was patient and well-behaved – no fuming and cursing like some of the spoiled animals there. In fact the vet said he was the 'best behaved' cat of the lot. The only thing was that he went off his food, and always came back thin.

Jack tells me that he would cry all the way home in his box, then, when arrived and let out, he would take one look round, and recognise where he was with a sigh of satisfaction: 'Home again!'

I wish I could have been there: I was never there for this part of the routine of his life, which I dictated from a distance. Jack adds – what goes to my heart: 'he had a lonely life at times'. Alas! – that he was loved so much, and deserted so much: irreparable now.

Was he spoiled?

I don't think so, for all that he was petted, not pampered. The Professor, old sobersides, thought that he was, and that he used to take advantage of me. But then the Professor didn't like cats, the only defect in an otherwise perfect character.

I don't blame him for not liking the Wow-wow, for she once gave him a terrible fright in the night, in my upstairs guest room at Polmear, by jumping in through the window upon the recumbent and sleeping Professor. It must have been as much of a surprise to her as it was to him – a live full Professor too!

Nor was the great authority on railway engines, who had been mad about puff-puffs since his own boyhood, at all amused by the variety of names this simple Cornish cat enjoyed.

I rather think at this time I was calling him Fanty, Fanty-cat, or Fantigue-cat – all breakaways, as the etymologists put it, from the Cardinal Infant. Hence, too, Twenty, or Twenty-cat. I don't know how that arrived; but with me words have always had their own life and inner motion, and I have played games with them from first to second childhood.

I suppose the Professor was allergic to the religion of Trenarren: Peter-worship. At Oxford, when we wondered why Bruce McFarlane never produced a book, Richard Pares put forward the view that if one penetrated into Bruce's rooms at Magdalen one would find him on his knees before the cat.

Certainly Peter recognised at once, when Bruce came to stay, that he knew about cats – unlike the Professor. Peter would lie in his lap and allow himself to be fondled in the way Bruce well knew how, when Peter would not obtrude himself upon the Professor.

His differing attitude to people expressed what he thought of them. He took Beryl more seriously than he did me – after all the more serious concerns of life revolved around her. She was the regular provider of food – I fed him at times, particularly at my own meal-times, but that was only when I was at home during vacations.

He would go for walks with her around the grounds, but not with me. Sometimes all three of us would go – and delightful it was, with him scampering on ahead, occasionally dashing madly up a tree, or lagging behind with the curious discontinuity of a cat. Except in the chase, when hunting or watching prey, they have less concentration than dogs. Hence people find their habit of not attending maddening, when they are bent on making a cat do something it doesn't want to do. People-who-know-about-cats know that you can't *make* a cat do anything – a point Douglas Jay long ago made to me; you may not even be able to persuade or entice or lure. Cats have their own will and personality – as Colette understood so well; they do not reflect the personality of their masters, as dogs do – though they may reflect, or conform, to their habits.

Peter hated it when Beryl was away from the house. If she went into town of an afternoon, he would see her off at the gate, hardly ever going beyond, but taking up his post by the gate to wait for her. Often there he still would be in the evening to welcome her back. When I was away, he would be waiting for her down in the paddock in the mornings. He recognised her footstep as she came up the steep road outside. He never jumped over the hedge, but would follow her progress from inside, saying 'Ma-ma' the while.

By the time she had arrived at the big black gate – which he never climbed over and rarely went through – there would be a tiny white nose peeping under the gap.

He had, indeed, a hundred pretty ways.

Both of us hated Saturdays, when Beryl was away all afternoon and evening. When evening came Peter would come into the study and take refuge on my lap. I comforted him and he comforted me; but when half-past nine came, it was no good – we both grew afraid, nerves and ears alert to every sound.

'Don't be late,' I would say; 'Peter doesn't like it.'

But I didn't like it either.

At last, he would receive the signal before me: he had heard the outside gate go, then the front door, and we would hear her steps in the hall.

'Beryl,' I would sing out, or more often, *'Béroul* – Peter wants to see you: he has been waiting and waiting.'

When Beryl came in, he would rouse himself to give her those two formal long licks the length of first and second fingers which represented the summit of his ritual of love – all with a lot of care and fuss and flurry. Never at other times, or in any other way.

'What about me?' I would say, sticking my first two fingers out, to receive the same ritual ablutions.

Once, in bed when my hand had got out over the coverlet, he woke me up with the same expressive gesture to tell me how much he loved me. Very endearing, and half asleep I responded by fondling head and ears as he liked.

At other times he has added to my nervousness. I have always been subject to night-terrors, and Cornish houses – if not precisely haunted – are distinctly atmospherical.

At a neighbouring old country house in mid-Cornwall, the squire was scribbling away in his study late at night, accompanied by his Esquimaux dog, window wide open. Suddenly the dog gave a loud howl and leaped through the window; nor did he return for three days.

Similarly with Peter; at one time he quite unnerved me two or three nights running by following something invisible along the cornice of the ceiling, right round the room.

Beryl said, 'Spiders.'

But one doesn't really know about extra-sensory perception, does one?

Later on, in his middle age, there came sickness. And in this he did follow his master (or servant), for he developed a stomach-ulcer and could keep nothing down.

Until this he had been a very healthy little creature, except for the tendency of cats to be chesty – one reason why the climate of Cornwall, warm and moist, is good for them, as with bronchial subjects.

When he had a cough, I used to smack him on the back or chest to help him – again, he knew it was for his good and would stand patiently to be smacked. After all, he was never smacked in anger (by me): he never needed it, as horrid children do or those half-grown children, university students.

'If the cat has but a cough, you are worried' – Beryl would laugh at me (as I occasionally am laughing at my readers).

But his first illness was no laughing matter for us, for he went and hid himself away, in the way sick animals do. We thought he was lost, and couldn't think what had happened to him. Another trap? Over the cliff? (quite near on the road side of the house). Poisoned?

I got it in my head that he was poisoned. For, when we lived in the hateful Council houses at Robartes Place in the midst of the I.P., we had an exquisite marmalade kitten, whom I brought home in my pocket and buttered my fingers for him to lick, according to custom, so that he would stay with us. He was dinky when he came; so I called him Dinky.

I was an undergraduate at Oxford then; and, while I was away, an odious working-man up across the way, poisoned all the cats that belonged there.

Is it any wonder that I simply hated living there with the idiot people? – but I was then too poor, and later on too ill, to make a move.

Beryl and I raised the hue and cry for our white cat. The third day the farmboy told us that a white cat had been seen up at Lobb's Shop – what must have been a blacksmith's shop long before my time, kept by the vanished Lobb, at the four turnings: to Trenarren and Trevissick (beautiful Queen Anne house, with Jacobean hall-kitchen), with Penrice and Porthpean along the road; to Pentewan, with haunted Sailors' Orchard on one side of the road, Polglaze of the Treleavens on the other; lastly, to Towan with its holy well, a rough track down through the King's Wood to Pentewan Valley.*

Beryl seized her stick and hurried up the lane, with me in hot pursuit. When we got up there, we discovered that the white cat seen there had been Farmer Yelland's from Castle Gotha.

No Peter!

Disconsolate we trudged back down Trenarren Lane, taking no notice of the wonderful views of the bay that open out along the road from Silvermine – right out to the Gribben on the other side from our Black Head.

Next morning I went out, and at the entrance to the back drive – there was Peter. Overjoyed, I took him up and covered him with kisses. He tried, but could hardly croak back in return.

I carried him down to my study, settled him in a warm rug in the chair by my desk and rang for the vet. There Peter remained, refusing food or milk, dozing, perfectly content to lie there beside me while I wrote.

The vet arrived – and waved aside my suggestion that he might have eaten something that poisoned him. Not a bit of it.

His temperature was taken – thermometer inserted in his

* Trenarren means the hamlet or house of the ploughed land, Trevissick that of the cornfield; Penrice, the head of the ford; Pentewan, the head of the sands; Porthpean, the little beach; Polglaze, the green pool; Towan, sands or sandy place; Gribben, the crest; Castle Gotha, the old round-camp.

rear without protest. His temperature was high – some fever, possibly pussy-cat flu.

The vet would give him a penicillin injection. I held him while the needle was inserted – a cry, but never a scratch or a bite.

By evening he was definitely better. I brought him a nice slice of chicken, which he consented to take rather coyly – then drank a whole saucer of water, which was what he liked.

He descended somewhat unsteadily from the chair, where he had lain passive all day, and went out of doors gaining strength and assurance with every step.

He was completely recovered.

CHAPTER SIX

My Absences in America

I think that, from the first, he liked the big house at Trenarren better than Polmear Mine – as we did. He didn't come into the house much there; but, after the move, he became more devoted to or dependent upon us, and lived with us far more. Trenarren became *his* place.

He explored all over the house and was more familiar with all its rooms than he had been at the smaller house. In the early days he would vanish upstairs for hours, we wondered where – and would come down covered with dust and blinking with cobwebs.

We thought he had been up a chimney. In fact he had discovered the exciting spaces, holes and corners, of the roof, haunt of bats, rafters festooned with spiders' webs. (I preserve the spiders and encourage their campaign against flies.)

One day when he came down from his exploration in this state, Beryl gave him a bath and, much to his disgust, dusted his coat with scented powder. He thought this rather sissy – but he certainly looked beautiful, ivory-white, with the distinguished ruff he had then, like an Elizabethan.

Cat-like, he disliked water in general, and I could never induce him to keep me company while I had a bath. Bruce's cat had no such allergy, and one day – such was his devotion – came and sat on Bruce's chest *in* the bath. Peter would not come near, nor stay on a chair beside me while I splashed about: he regarded the spectacle as horrid, mewing the whole time with apprehension.

When we first came to the house I used to make morning-tea off the electric point in my bedroom. But he could not bear the sizzling noise of the kettle: it always disturbed him, probably affected his sensitive ears. Not all my wooing, or explaining, 'Make-a-tea, make-a-tea', persuaded him.

He knew the cellars better than I did, or have ever done. They continue all round under the house, excellent roomy compartments, cobbled or flagged, with at one point blocked-up stone steps that would arrive at the front door. At another a stone gives the date of the foundation, 1805, the year of Trafalgar.

They are quite big enough to stow away a regiment of soldiers. And must have stowed away many a cask of brandy, brought ashore from the cove on Black Head – Q. has a smuggling story of the lane out from the ledra to the headland and beach.

Then there are slate pans for brining the bacon, vaults for storing the wine, the coals that in old days were brought up over the cliff from Ropehawn,* where there was a little quay, now vanished. In fact, all the storage necessary for those days with family, servants, a household which, marooned out on this headland, needed to be self-sufficient.

In my time, a vast prowling place for Peter. Dr Johnson called the Codrington Library at All Souls a fine place to prance in. I never followed Peter on his prancing expeditions, keeping the mice down for us – but once, when he disappeared again for two or three days, found him with a cold nursing himself on the window-sill beside the stove down below that supplied central heating.

As for mice – if Beryl ever had a mouse in the kitchen, we simply shut Peter in for the night. There in the morning would be our mouse laid out for us on the mat. He well understood the approbation and praises he received: '*Good* cat! caught the *Mouse*', etc.

He hadn't the courage of a tom-cat and, naturally, having been neutered, was a bit sissy. Beryl used to say that he had 'a pretty face for a tom-cat'; I used to demur at this. Now I think she was right: he had a delicate, shapely head, with exquisite pink-transparent ears, like shell-whorls, nice whiskers and pale gentle eyes with a kind welcoming expres-

* Ropehawn = Ropehaven.

54

sion. For he had been loved into a state of perpetual seduction – I had only to put out a hand and he would purr. What a welcome always awaiting one!

I think that, among the small number of words he knew, was the word 'love': he knew it not in the abstract sense but in the concrete meaning of being loved.

There was, for example, the chair in the dining room by the window, where he was accustomed to being loved. This meant kisses on the forehead, where were the diminutive pretty furrows; rubbing noses like Polynesians – a gesture of equality much appreciated by cats from humans; then nuzzling into his flank: an occasional squeak of protest and pleasure at being hugged too hard; then, subsidence into deep sleep. I would pull the curtain forward to protect him from the sun, and he would sleep there the whole morning.

The fact is that cats are mesmerisable. John Opie, the Cornish painter, would vary the occupation – for which he was scolded by his unresponsive, stupid parent – of 'for ever dra'in the cat', by mesmerising it.

What a subject! – the enchanting paintings of cats, by Hogarth, Gainsborough and other artists – and an exacting subject too, to catch their changing expressions and delicate gestures – that marvellous flick of the back leg, for example, to shake off a raindrop. Then there are the drawings of Beatrix Potter, or Louis Wain, who went off his head about cats. (I well understand that.)

To understand the mind, and world, of a cat would be a difficult and subtle task – beyond the barbarous methods of a physiologist like Pavlov – for, to begin with, there is their double life: their life with us, and their secret life to themselves, away from humans.

How many words did Peter know?

Not many – not so many as Barney (up in Trelawny Road), for he was not a clever cat; and no cats know as many words as dogs, for they are less dependent on humans, and dogs have larger brains.

I think all animals are not only responsive to the human voice but fascinated by it – for them the one marked difference between them and us, with our command of every variety of expression: it is through the voice that we command them, direct them, entice them, scold them, make them love or fear us, teach them. I find very touching the effort the poor creatures make to follow our words, enter into our not always clear wishes, sometimes emitting a little squeak, like a question. They seem to be proud of themselves when they succeed in catching our meaning.

Peter knew the word Beryl; and Dinner; I think he knew the words Mouse, and Milk. Also No, and Out? He would go over to door or window, while I said Out? It seems that it is more by tone of voice, and association that a cat will recognise a word, or a command.

Did he know the word Tea, or Cake? – I rather think he knew the latter; he had a special fondness for sponge-cake, which he would eat out of my hand, stickily licking up the crumbs left over. In fact, he was keen to pick up crumbs once pointed out.

Not having much courage was in itself a measure of defence. He never put himself in the way of danger and kept away from strangers. But he had the regular animal sense of his own territory and didn't like incursions into it – by the farm-cats for instance. When I have been shooing one off the lawn he would accompany me, making a pretence of courage and saying Gr-r – so long as I was beside him.

Once down in the orchard, when I was speaking kind words to a farm-cat that dared to approach me, Peter growled angrily, overcome by jealousy: I was *his* property. I told him that he was no better than a human – which made him look properly ashamed.

However, I did not put too great a strain on his good nature by praising another cat in his presence – as Dr Johnson did in front of his Hodge. Seeing the look of reproach on Hodge's face, the great bear of a Doctor with the tender heart, hastily added, 'But Hodge is a good cat, too' – and all was well.

Now were to come the bad times when I took to going more and more to America; for that meant no Christmas vacation at home, and no Christmas fare for him. Wherever I was I thought of him so much that I often fancied I heard his voice in the night, when in bed at my hotel on Seventh Avenue in New York, in my penitential cell at the Athenaeum in Pasadena, in the restricted quarters to which I consigned myself at Urbana, Illinois, or Madison, Wisconsin; in the loneliness of hotels in Chicago, San Francisco, Philadelphia, Boston (when I might have been in my rooms at All Souls or at home at lovely Trenarren. There I would be awakened by a seagull's cry, often thinking it was Peter outside on the terrace below.)

Crossing to Canada in *The Empress of Britain* in 1957, 'I distinctly heard three mews of the p.l.f. in the night. I do hope you are loving him a little in my absence. I put you in my will *on condition you did*.'

Evidently from the letters Beryl kept, and all the money I sent for him month by month, I did what I could to have him looked after – and Beryl faithfully preserved him for me, though nothing could make up for my long absences.

But I can't go into all the references to him in the pocket note-books I kept when away – too much like historical research. The letters Beryl kept almost all send messages to Peter. 'Hug my p.l. cat for me: I think of him often.' P.l. stood for poor little, and from this time he became P.L.F., or poor little fellow; sometimes, poor little angel; or 'glad to hear that the little Saint remains well and sensible'. Every month the letters send extra money for his keep, to vary the tins of meat for his diet, or for milk and fish.

From the Athenaeum in California, October 1962: 'I dare

say P.L.F. is in need of a few more tins for the month – milk and the stuff he likes from Mr. Dunn's (the florist, about whom I wrote a story). Jack calls the P.L.F. – D.L.F. (dear little fellow) and I think he is. I miss him very much, but have started a new book and am working hard.' This was my biography of Shakespeare. But how dreadful it was to have to leave the poor little fellow.

One winter crossing on board the *Queen Elizabeth* – January 1959, on my way to Madison, Wisconsin – there were two bad days with the ship doing a corkscrew motion. Never a good sailor (why, O why was I going?), 'I spent the time in bed with a sore head, thinking how Peter would like it. If he were on board he would go frantic, and jump into the Atlantic. You can tell him that the *Queen Elizabeth* is an enor*mouse* ship.'

Pretty regularly there is a present enclosed for 'the poor little fellow alone for hundreds of hours'. This was what was so sad – to have made him so fond of me and then to have deserted him (like Trenarren itself) most of the time. I don't know what he thought, but he became a sadder little cat as he grew older, accepting it stoically – needs must, as I had to myself.

I thought of him every day of my life, as I still do, particularly going to bed and getting up in the morning If there is such a thing as extra-sensory perception, then he knew that I was thinking of him.

But what was the good of that? Well, perhaps it helped a little – it certainly helped me. But did it help him? One letter says, 'I am thinking of him, as I hope he is thinking of me.' Who knows how much he did in those hundreds of hours alone. Beryl says he had 'hard times' when I was away – as I was now most of the time.

She also says that I had more patience with him than she had, and infinitely more patience with him than with humans – for whom I have none. After all, they ought to know better. She tells me that I used to say that he never provoked or answered back, but was grateful for whatever was done for him.

To adapt Swift: Only a little cat.

I took to enclosing a letter for him – a piece of light-weight paper, on which I rubbed my hand. Beryl said that he would take notice and sniff at it, recognise that it was a message from me to him.

Here is the next winter in California, December 1963. 'Last night I was dreaming of Trenarren, and poor little Peter. (Perhaps another way of being in contact?) I dreamed he was a little tabby, and small and thin. So I am sending him a little letter for him to smell that I am still alive and £1 for the tinned stuff that he likes.'

When I was away Beryl went down to her cottage at night. Another letter again suggests, 'If you feel lonely at night, why don't you take Peter down every evening? He would like it – he is very lonely in the house and would be nice company, and also catch the mouse.'

Beryl was not fond of cats or dogs (but, incomprehensibly, of children); however, she became attached to Peter, he had such endearing ways, and perhaps because I was so devoted to him. My letters try to persuade her to have him with her at the cottage, on the ground that he would be good company for her: 'I find him so' (and it would be company for him).

Cats are the perfect companions for a writer: they are so quiet and unobtrusive, not for ever demanding attention like dogs, or having to be taken for walks. Peter would lie curled up beside me for hours, while I was engaged in the inexplicable occupation of pushing a pen.

There was one exception: he did not like the upstairs study, I never could understand why. Downstairs study, library, my bedroom, were all right; but in the upstairs study he would get restless, and even sit mewing disconsolately at the door.

Why? Was it draughty? Or ghosty? Was there perhaps a Presence?

For me this was disappointing, for it is my favourite room : silent, away from the goings on, the inevitable noises, in the house; window open to the view of the magical valley, the bay, the line of Trenarren beeches; across the lawn to his favourite post as a young hunter, where I think I see him still, dear white shade against the green bank.

When the Victorian additions at the back of the house were being pulled down, I knew he would hate the noise and fuss, and he took to going down to the cottage more with Beryl. He never came to the front door there – cats are such routineers – but mewed at the back door. He came and sat by the fire with her all the evening, but never stayed all night. He would either go across to the shed on the other side of the lane, or go back to the house.

Often they were to be seen mounting the hill together in the mornings on their way back to the big house. Of course I would worry about passing motor-cars in the narrow lane, but I think that when alone he went sagely up and down his own way, via the garden, kitchen garden and orchard, safe most of the way. Jack would report to me about his well-being, and now there were friends from Oxford who had fallen for the Valley.

'I had such a nice letter from Mr Hartley to say that Peter was looking better. *What* kind people they are! He knew that was the way to my heart. So perhaps we shall be able to keep p.l.f. for a year or two yet. (Some people are perfect fools about their animals – especially dogs.)'

The little cat had been ill – I hope it wasn't from grief, though cutting his life in two with such a marked difference, the love he got when I was there and then the long absences, cannot have been good for him. Difference of diet, too – living

on the fat of the land with me; then a horrid diet of tinned
cats' food. His sickness took the form of an ulcer; he couldn't
keep his food down. We called in the vet, who prescribed
tablets for him. I was there as always in the summer, and
helped to treat him.

He was angelic about taking his pills. I would open his
mouth without the least fuss, pop the pill in, and hold his
mouth shut until he had swallowed it. Never the slightest
struggle let alone biting or scratching – he never bit or
scratched anyone in his life: he seemed to *know*.

He was a submissive little creature. On some later
occasions, when I had to hold him for a penicillin injection,
I would give him a kiss before and after in the hope of telling
him that it was intended for his good – difficult for a poor
creature to appreciate. But how trusting, and confiding!
Such trust is very touching – as a truly great man, Sherrington the physiologist, says in a wonderful book, *Man on
his Nature*. It is all the more heart-breaking to think of such
trust being betrayed (but wasn't I betraying it myself?), and
the inequity of man's cruelty to animals.

Homo homini lupus, but I cannot bear to think of man's
cruelty to animals – horses in war, in the bull-ring, pit-ponies
living their lives underground – for they, poor creatures, are
not responsible.

Now I had to leave home again. From California next
month, November 1961: 'I am glad he has taken to living
down there with you in the evenings – he is very nice company. I am sending him £2 for extra food.' Next month, 'I
am very pleased indeed that you have got Peter round his
illness. I am sure it is the milk that has done it – very healing
for ulcers.' (I was an old subject myself.) 'So I am sending
£2.'

Enclosing a 'contribution to your Christmas feast – very
glad you are going down with your father for Christmas. I
am sure P. will be all right at the vet's for four days. Yes,
he is very devoted to you. I miss him a great deal here and

often think of him. However, I am getting on splendidly with my book – nothing else to do but write every day at the Library from 9 to 5.'

Back in Oxford, 'I keep thinking of my poor little cat shut up at the vet's. Is he getting better?'

From Canada, stopping with Beaverbrook at Fredericton: 'it was comforting to know that all is well at Tre, especially with Peter. I miss him dreadfully, and think of him every night going to bed. However, where I dined last night they had a nice cat with very nice ways.'

Arrived in California, 'enquiries *here* for P.L.F. today – he's internationally famous'. True it is, there were regular inquiries for him, not only at Oxford, where quite a lot of people who had stayed at Trenarren knew him and others who knew of him, but also in California from Allan and Mary Nevins, Robert and Margaret Dougan, Robert Wark who knew Trenarren, so too did Margaret and Ward Swain of Urbana, besides friends in New York and elsewhere who knew about him.

If only he had known! – humble little soul that he was.

But I was glad to hear that he recognised the letters I sent him, and hoped at another time that he knew I was coming. At another, 'I am longing to see him.'

This was the simple truth. As I drove home from Oxford, the thought of seeing him again possessed my mind more and more. Sounding the horn from Lobb's Shop round all the corners of Trenarren Lane – I think he recognised the note from all other cars. He knew when I sounded a few gentle toots all for him, sitting back safe and smug among the flowers of the front bed – Beryl's bed. He sat there with an expression of satisfaction and recognition that it was meant for him – almost as if he had a sense of humour and were smiling.

It certainly seems that dogs can laugh, baring their teeth, perhaps in imitation of their human deities. Where dogs laugh, cats smile – or at any rate wear that Cheshire-cat expression of smug awareness, as when Barney skimmed the cream-jug.

And I think both dogs and cats are grateful to those humans who take the trouble to amuse them; they have so much time on their hands, or, perhaps I should say, paws.

The first day at home, he would be lying on the floor in the kitchen between Beryl at the sink and me at the door, I would inquire loudly:

'Has Peter been a good cat? Did he look after his Beryl?'

He would know that we were talking about him and would purr as loudly back. I would then slip my foot out of my slipper and roll him over, rubbing his belly. He would claw my stockinged foot with pleasure till it hurt, and Beryl would scold, 'Stop it, Peter!'

At once he took notice of what she said. He wasn't supposed to be in the Library; if she caught him on the sofa and shouted 'Off it, Peter!', he dashed off and under a chair at once. When I said, 'Now you naughty cat, you know you are not supposed to be on the sofa,' she says: 'He wouldn't move for you: you used to pick him up so gentle.'

By the same token as I approached the house with joy at the thought of seeing him again, of course it always made me miserable to leave him. I knew so well that grey look of misery round his eyes – as I knew that look of absolute fidelity and devotion with which he looked at me when he was happy. (Bruce once spoke to me of the look in his cat's eyes – what insensitive rubbish people talk of cats not being loving, or even being less loving than dogs!)

The trouble is the reverse: they can be too loving and faithful. Then, as with all love, one is vulnerable and liable to suffer.

Knowing his misery from the moment he knew I was due to leave, a day or so before, I would be quite upset at leaving, drive out at the gate in the grey of morning – tears in our eyes, both Beryl and I – and off up the lane, heavy at heart, up and up the steep hills through the china clay area of my childhood, across Bodmin Moor, setting my face towards work and duty, Oxford and America.

CHAPTER SEVEN

P.L.F.

Peter was growing old now. One summer at home I wrote
a poem about him, with the old Irish poem, 'Banur Dan',
in mind and with the refrain,

My cat and I grow old together.

A number of people have noticed it, though never
mentioned, of course, by those discouragers of poetry, con-
temporary critics.* (They have helped largely to kill the liking for poetry among the public.)

Now we are too often apart, yet
Turning out of Central Park into the Plaza,
Or walking Michigan Avenue against the lake-wind,
I see a little white shade in the shrubbery
Of far-off Trenarren, never far from my mind.

Towards Christmas-time in California, 1964, I send money
'for P.L.F.'s tins – perhaps Jack will bring some down that
will give him a change, something he likes. I think of him
every day. I suppose he is thirteen now. Terrible. P.L.F.'

But he continued a few years yet, the next year 'I was
glad to hear that P.L.F. was better and stronger. Perhaps
that was the effect of his good diet in the summer. I hope
he doesn't get too run down in the winter, now he can't catch
birds and mice.'

For Christmas Beryl sent me some snaps. 'They made me
feel quite homesick – especially to see Peter looking round

---

* It has since been put, though not the best of my poems, into the *Oxford Book
of Twentieth Century Verse.*

as if looking for me. And I am away from him so much when I shan't have him for much longer.'

One of those last summers I found Peter had struck up a friendship with a poor little ginger-cat who was a stray: I was glad of this, it mitigated Peter's loneliness a bit.

Poor 'Ginger', as I called him, had met with some terrible injury at human hands; his chest was gashed as if by a rock thrown at him, and no inducement would ever persuade him to come near a human again.

He was starving, and I used to carry out food for him. He was afraid of a plate as of a trap, poor creature; so I carried food to some corner, where he could take it while in shelter.

He grew to know my call, 'Ginger, Ginger', and would always answer me, pitifully, his small voice coming from the shrubberies.

Peter didn't like me talking to the poor creature too much, and for this I reproached him: 'Poor Ginger.'

In any case Ginger would never come near a human – what can he have suffered at their hands? And when I next came home, without me there to feed him, he had disappeared for ever.

At New York, from California, 'I was so pleased to hear of the P.L.F.'s good behaviour, waiting for you up in a tree all the afternoon.' So I sent him money for his tins of meat and a present to Beryl for looking after him so well.

She was becoming more attached to him and he to her.

I deserved to take only second place, I was away the greater part of the year, at Oxford or in America. But Beryl says that, when I came home, he became my cat.

True, I was the provider, earning the money for his upkeep and that of Trenarren, and I thought of him constantly, did what I could to have him looked after from afar.

But – so like life and love – I was failing him. I was too little at home: he was becoming Beryl's cat.

I wasn't jealous: I was only too glad that, since I was so much away, she had at last become fond of the poor little fellow.

But how love finds one out, searches out one's failings, convicts one of inadequacy. It is true, and I am ashamed to own it, that as he grew older, less beautiful and beguiling, feebler and less attractive and perhaps needed love more, I loved him less.

Isn't that so like life, the perhaps ineluctable failing of the human being, with which I now reproach myself?

Yet, in growing old and frail, he set so much better an example than most humans can do, than anything I can hope for in my turn as I approach my end.

As his faculties failed him, once more the instinctive wisdom of the poor creature made its adaptation. As his hearing failed him, he would take up his station from a position whence he could see what was happening either at the front or back door.

Across from the front door he had a comfortable nest under the great pine-tree. From here he could see if I were having a meal out on the terrace. Sometimes, when he was too tired or feeble, I would take up his saucer of milk or water as he lay there.

At night, when I went out, with some trepidation, into the dark shrubberies to call him in, 'Peter Rowse, Peter Rowse!', he would answer me and come to me, tail up, and I'd pick him up in my arms, to spare his paws on the sharp gravel.

Beryl used to laugh at the care with which I used to set him down, not let him jump down on the gravel.

We used to summon him outdoors by clapping our hands, sometimes making such a noise when he didn't come, we would be heard all over Trenarren. Beryl would say people must think we're dotty – little did I care what they thought, thinking what I did of them!

Once when there was a torrential downpour and he was

sheltering under a shrub across from the back door, we clapped and called and shouted to him to come in out of the rain. It took him a long time to risk wetting his feet (like Wilson Steer as a special constable in Chelsea in the 1914–18 war).

At last he made a dash for it – to be welcomed by me with a warm cloth and rubbed all over, paws and all. Protesting at the tickling parts of the process, his purr rose to a roar of pleasure.

Beryl: 'This cat is better looked after than some children.'

To this observation I would regularly tease back: 'But, you see, he's *so* much more beautiful. And *much* nicer.'

No crying and stamping and squealing and tempers as with them.

To all this I used to say, 'He has given us his heart: we have an absolute obligation to look after him.' Yet I feel that I failed him at the last – the innate inadequacy of human nature.

Yet I did substitute for calling to him in his last years going round the shrubberies flashing a torch: he recognised that and would come along.

Even towards the end, when he grew thin and poor, neglected himself and had lost his beauty, when I told him he was beautiful, the poor little fellow would perk up, summon up his feeble strength to lick and clean himself and look his best.

Most of the time, he was sleeping his life away, appetite failing him.

I was failing him. I no longer wanted to have him in bed with me. Once, on my last visit home, when he wanted to lie in my lap, as in the old days, I rejected him: he lay on the arm of the loved arm-chair as close as he could nestle to the warmth of my arm. There's human inadequacy! I cannot forgive myself.

Yet, when I came down in the early morning to make the tea, he would be lying just outside the kitchen door; when

I put out my foot to pat him, he would immediately clasp my foot and begin to purr. (Like Hardy's blinded bird – 'Who thinketh no evil, but sings.'

I knew we could not keep him much longer. On my arrival in California in October 1966, 'I had a pleasant welcome from two Pasadena cats this morning: a very affectionate Siamese, like poor Bruce's Jasper, who ran away when Bruce died; and a Blue Persian with thick fur.'

At New Year I wrote that I was longing to see him, and when I returned to Oxford in March there was a hope that I might. Then something detained me, and I was too late. Beryl said that he was waiting and waiting to see me, but he could hold out no longer.

I was glad not to be there to see his end, I could not have borne it.

Fortunately Beryl was not alone in the house; Geoffrey Hudson was staying there, to recuperate from an illness. He knew and was fond of Peter: it was a great stay that he was there. The poor little fellow had an eminent Orientalist to his burying.

She could not tell me about his end when I telephoned; she wrote me a letter, which she then did not send, but waited to tell me when I came. 'I couldn't tell you this on the telephone, I should be too upset. Our P.L.F. is gone, after sixteen years. I tried to keep him for you, but it wasn't to be.'

He was dying, but I think he was waiting for me to come home. He was lying in a box in the passage inside the back door, where we had shut him at night those first few days at Trenarren. He was old and smelly and could no longer clean himself. People came to see Beryl – he hadn't been out for a couple of days, so she sent him out at the back door; and when he tried to come back, shut him out.

When the end of the day came, he was nowhere to be found. It was March and cold. Geoffrey huddled on his coat, and 'we searched everywhere, indoors and out, up the stables, top field, down the engine house, paddocks, under rhodo bushes, everywhere we could think of'. When Jack came next day, he searched too. 'We thought he had gone to die in one of his favourite places, such as the bank opposite your bathroom-window, or over under the old fir tree, or in my flower-bed by the gate. We looked everywhere, the places we knew he liked.'

Then Jack thought of the cottage. There he was in the shed across the road, where he used to wait for Beryl, lying with tail up with the friendly greeting he always had for us both – just as if, at the last, he had seen someone he loved.

All the last offices fell to Beryl. I had escaped, as usual, the obligations of love I can hardly support. I was relieved not to be there at the end; those three days that I was overdue saved me – but I had failed him. 'I am glad you did not see him, remember him as you knew him, a constant and loyal friend.'

She made a little shroud for him, and they buried him in the upper field, away from the house – so that I should not be constantly reminded if I knew where nearby – the 'field' which had been the kitchen-garden in old days, and which he knew both by day and by night as I have never done.

'Mr. Chappell, Mr. Hudson and me took him to his last resting-place. Mr. Chappel dug his grave, I placed him in it and said, "Goodbye, Peter." Mr. Hudson and I were very sad. Sixteen years is a long life for a cat, so we mustn't grieve for him, although I am missing him very much. I have shed many tears I can tell you to think he looked for me and could not find me. Mr. Hudson was such a help, I was glad he was here.'

But I was not there. What had kept me away – something instinctive?

Mustn't grieve for him, indeed! – I grieve for him always.

It is over five years since he left us, and – though I have always intended to write his life, along with the rest of them, I have had the greatest difficulty in doing so, even now, though I have put it off so long.

Ordinary people, good friends, have told me that I ought at once to have filled the gap he left with another cat – and, in one way, no doubt they are right. But my feelings are Hardy's, who could not bring himself to have another cat after the one he so much loved:

> Never another pet for me
> Let your place all vacant be;
> Better blankness day by day
> Than companion torn away.
> Better bid his memory fade,
> Better blot each mark he made,
> Selfishly escape distress
> By contrived forgetfulness,
> Than preserve his prints to make
> Every morn and eve an ache.

But yet, one cannot 'selfishly escape distress' or contrive forgetfulness either – there is the nexus in which one is caught, the inescapable condition of life.

> From the chair whereon he sat
> Sweep his fur, nor wince thereat;
> Rake his little pathways out
> Mid the bushes roundabout;
> Smooth away his talons' mark
> From the claw-worn pinetree bark,
> Where he climbed as dusk embrowned
> Awaiting us who loitered round.

Hardy was filled with the sense of life's ironies, and he knew well that one cannot do those things: one cannot forget. I still find little bits of Peter's white fur in unexpected places; on old coats there are the claw-marks where he would cling to my shoulder, on trouser-legs the tiny mementoes of his attracting my attention, as if I would ever forget him or leave him out.

Then Hardy goes on to reflect on the strangeness of it all –

> Strange it is this speechless thing,
> Subject to our mastering,
> Subject for his life and food
> To our gift, and time, and mood;
> Timid pensioner of us Powers,
> His existence ruled by ours,
> Should – by crossing at a breath
> Into safe and shielded death,
> By the merely taking hence
> Of his insignificance –

become significant, become part of the mystery, in fact at that point join with us.

For the life of a little cat has its significance just as the life of a man – shares in the miracle of birth, the redeeming spirit of love, the mystery of death.

There is a moving passage in a book by one of the great spirits of our time, the physiologist Sherrington, *Man on his Nature*, a key-book for me, since it represents what I believe myself.

After giving an account of man's evolution into man, with the achievement of the roof-brain – the latest and most complex mechanism in nature – with the accompanying development of love and loyalty, altruism and self-sacrifice, the characteristics that make man what he is, or can be, and marks him off from the animals, Sherrington goes on to say that among the higher creatures of animal life there are those that have struggled upwards to share in these attributes and also show love and friendship and fidelity. So that we have an obligation to them, poor creatures, as to ourselves.

This thought speaks for me. Though it was not on account of any such intellectual consideration that I cared for Peter so much: I suppose, for me, he was an element of love in a somewhat unloving life, or at any rate a life that held love at bay. Love involves suffering: there is the inextricable nexus of life, the tragic fate of man, for which religion seeks to provide consolation.

Nor again are philosophic reflections, Hardy's or mine, necessary to account for the love I felt for Peter. He was so much part of our life at Trenarren. Among the many names I called him he was sometimes the 'little spirit', or 'little soul'. For, indeed, he was the spirit of the place.

Beryl summed it up, when she said to me today: 'He lived with us so many years, he was like a member of the family.' Which, of course, he was for me: Beryl and Jack, Peter and me: our little family.

He came with us to Trenarren, he loved it there, he spent those best years with us, for we too are growing old.

Everybody knew about him: I suppose people took notice of him because they knew I loved him so much. All my friends, at Oxford and in America, asked for him – some of them still do, though it is years afterwards.

Hardy wrote tenderly:

> Housemate, I can think you still
> Bounding to the window-sill,
> Over which I vaguely see
> Your small mound beneath the tree,
> Showing in the autumn shade
> That you moulder where you played.

He would never possess another cat.

But 'possess'? We possess nothing, we inhabit our own loneliness.

There is no mound here, and – come to think of it – that is a bit materialist of Hardy. For, wherever I am in the house I can yet see that dear white shade – a familiar figure in most rooms of the big house; every window or door downstairs I have often opened to let him in or out; in the garden I see him in his favourite nooks or nests, sniffing at a flower or just tickling his nose with it, or posted across the lawn whence he could look up at the window where I was writing – as I am writing now about him.

Within, the house is rather empty without him; outside, in the garden, there is a certain loneliness.

PART TWO

Chalky Jenkins:
A Little Cat Lost

He came in at the big upper gate on an afternoon when I was working at the border. It must have been autumn, or end of the summer vacation, for I was raking leaves out of the bed. He had followed Jack, my helper in the garden, in from the road. Jack had noticed a little white cat astray, on his own, looking for something to amuse him.

He was hardly more than a kitten still, perhaps three parts grown, for he was of a small species – small delicate head, very dainty and spotless. He was all white, except for the tiniest touch of tabby on his forehead, by which I should know him still among a hundred cats.

He was very circumspect and almost deferential at first – coming into the big place, with a couple of strange men at work – and I came to know that that was characteristic of him. He had *very* good manners. He asked permission to play.

I stroked him very gently, less hard than he had expected or could have wished – and that is one clue to making friends with a cat: no roughness or brusqueness. Let them know that they are welcome, then let them do the running, for they are apt to be subtle animals – not obvious and bouncy, like dogs.

He at once recognised someone who knew about cats, himself made the pace, weaved himself in and out between my legs, and was shortly having a fine game with the leaves, following the rake with quick fascinated movements, making little runs and pounces with out-stretched white paw.

All in inverted commas, of course. For, another thing about cats, they know that it is not wholly serious: they have a sense of humour; they pretend. Fascinated by movements of rake and leaves, watching, pouncing, crouching, withdrawing, giving up – for, after all, it is only a game.

For me, he was an answer to prayer. I had long missed Peter, the cat of my life, dead now four or five years; and this little cat that had suddenly appeared was white like Peter. But not a long-haired Persian: short-haired, with no such beautiful plume of a tail, rather stumpy in fact; and, as I was to learn, very different in temperament.

But where had he come from? Whose was he? He had arrived on me from nowhere – could he become mine?

Gardening finished, I took him into the house and gave him a saucer of milk. This was accepted – a difference from Peter, who was always a bit difficult about milk, and actually preferred water. But the little cat was not interested in food, not hungry: had obviously come from some home where he was well cared-for.

I couldn't keep him, just like that. Beryl, boss of indoor domestic arrangements, said that he belonged 'down the village', the hamlet of half-a-dozen houses in the valley below the big house.

So down he had to be taken, to the gate at the bottom end of the garden, where he seemed to know his whereabouts and whence he made his way home.

The next time I was at home from Oxford he appeared again, always when someone opened the upper gate. It does not seem to have occurred to him to crawl under the gate or to climb over the wall.

There he was again, in that attitude in which I shall always remember him: back to the hedge of the back-drive, tail up inquiringly, not in any way obsequious but just wondering about his reception. (I say 'always', but, alas, I saw him only half-a-dozen times altogether.)

This time I knew his name, and that surprised him. He was called Chalky, and belonged – if that is the word for it – to a young family of newcomers down in the village. They had brought him with them; their little girl, who had been fond of him, was now away at school, and the young couple were away for days at a stretch. Though they left food for him outside the door, he was on the loose; neglected, though not starved, still not much more than a kitten, half or three-quarters grown. Left to fend for himself. Chalky Jenkins.

I took him up in my arms, called him by his name; he leaped on to my shoulders, rubbing against my head, purring hardly audibly. (Another contrast with Peter, who purred like a traction-engine). Setting him down inside the front door, I coosed* him along the hall to the kitchen, he turning round to see if I was there all right and skidding on the polished floor, just as Peter used to do.

He knew his way to the kitchen, where the milk was and also supper, which I got Beryl to give him.

But she wouldn't keep him in the house: he belonged to the Jenkinses, and it wasn't fair to entice him away, leaving him on his own when I went back to Oxford, i.e. for *her* to look after. I well understood the situation, and indeed it *was* unfair to attach him to me when he belonged to somebody else, and then leave him on his own when I went away.

I took him to the back door and put him out. When I sat down to my supper in the dining-room, he found his way round to the front, and came pathetically putting his paws up to the window, mewing to come in.

That was too much for me and, knowing that I was doing wrong, I let him in and took him off to bed with me.

He knew all about going to bed, sat composedly inside my bedroom door, cleaning himself, making his toilet, but keeping an eye on me. When I was ready, I picked him up: he knew how to fit into the cosy little nest between the pillows and my neck, where the eiderdown came up and half covered him.

This was what he wanted. Before settling in for the night he gave my finger just one grateful lick – the only one I was

* Cornish for chased, half in fun.

ever to receive from him – just as Peter would do: one, and no more.

His bed-manners were perfect. He never moved the whole night – where Peter was apt to take more than his share of the bed and lie right across me, or begin to fuss to go out hunting in the middle of the night.

This little cat was very well brought up: no fussing, no trouble. I occasionally awoke and petted him, when there would be the faintest purr, a light murmur – perhaps he wasn't old enough to purr properly.

But when we both awoke and came down to breakfast, there was a fuss from Beryl. It wasn't 'fair', it wasn't 'right'. Nor was it. I took him down through the garden on my shoulders – he holding on to the manner born, thinking it a good spree, unsuspecting his betrayal – put him outside the bottom gate and shut it, leaving him alone in the lane to find his way home.

He did not try to climb the wall and follow me back; but I shall not forget the look of mute reproach in his eyes.

Friends of mine coming to the house – the discriminating ones who would notice a cat – had caught sight of him. Frances and Nicholas Kendall over from Pelyn asked me if I hadn't got a new cat in place of the adored Peter. I told them the story, that I should like to adopt him, but wasn't allowed to, etc.

'But don't you see, dear A. L., it isn't a question of your adopting him: *he's* adopting *you*.'

I explained that I couldn't keep him, that he belonged to people in the village.

'But he has chosen *you*. Cats do, you know. You can't possibly not have him.'

They, too, knew that he was just what I wanted: a little white cat to take the place of Peter. (They knew how I had grieved for *him*, how much I missed him from Trenarren, always waiting for me when I came home from Oxford, New

York, California. He knew the sound of the hoot of my car – and I always hooted for him coming round Trevissick Corner and down Trenarren Lane. But he knew intuitively that I was on my way, without these premonitory signals. My heart always went faster as I rounded these last corners, with the thought of seeing him. Now no-one.)

It seems disloyal to say so, but young Chalky had one or two advantages over old Peter. For one thing, he was gayer, more eager and amusing. There was something a little sad about Peter: he was such a lonely cat. He gave his love to me, and I was away much more than half of the time – three-quarters of the year latterly, when spending winters in California.

For another thing, Peter was easily frightened: he hadn't much confidence in life. The new little cat, though not so beautiful, was more spirited, had such an eager confidence in life, was capable of fending for himself (Peter was not).

But was this wholly an advantage, I reflected. Peter kept in around the grounds – a paradise for a cat – and hardly ever wandered out on the roads. *This* poor little cat was left on the roads, would take a ride with anybody in a car. (Peter couldn't be persuaded to enter a car.) I was a bit concerned lest the cars scooting up and down our narrow lane mightn't run over Chalky. It didn't occur to me that someone might equally pop him into their car and away with him – since it hadn't been likely with Peter.

The next time Chalky turned up was a gala-day for him: televising going on in the house.

I was having to do a turn with Colin Wilson, a long interview about my poetry. The library was turned inside-out and upside-down, furniture thrown out into the hall, piled up in corners to make a cosy bogus hearth-side scene; a crew of eight or nine technicians, cameramen, men to do the lights, connect up with the van in the back court, producer, controller of Westward TV, secretary, what not. Huge arc-lamps, two menacing, moving cameras, cables, wires, wires everywhere, you had to be careful where to put a foot down.

In the midst of it all arrived Chalky. Somebody must have told him down in the village that something interesting was going on up at the big house – or perhaps, by this time, that life was always more amusing up there than at the cottage with his people for ever going away.

So up he came to lend a hand. And a fine old time he had. Peter would have run away into the backwoods at the racket going on. Not so Chalky: he put his nose into everything, marched up and down amongst everybody, inquiring into this or that, tail up, in and out the wires. When things began to hot up, I was afraid he might be electrocuted.

So, before the performance began, he had to be shut away in the glory-hole at the back, where he slept peacefully through all the proceedings: not a mew. Very well-behaved, knowing little cat.

When it was all over, and peace restored to the household, I determined to take him right down the hill to his people and tell them to look after him better. He rode joyfully on my shoulders down that bumpy hill to the cottage, but it was all shut-up and desolate, nobody at home, the little cat's plate and saucer indeed outside the door but empty, licked clean.

Across the way were my Oxford friends, Joan and Harold, kindhearted and considerate to all creatures (even human). They told me the situation – how this exquisite little creature, beautifully mannered, brought up to be loved, wanting affection above all, was left for days on end loose on the roads.

I grew warm, in fact, furious. I remembered how frequently in America people would move house, leave the vicinity completely – and abandon their cat, a castaway, to starve and be hunted down. *Odious* humans, their irresponsibility, their thoughtlessness, taking on a poor creature dependent on them, then cruelly throwing it over. All my hatred of humans, for their sheer idiocy, surged up: I left a pretty hot message to be delivered to the young couple when they came back to the cottage.

I left Chalky on his own deserted doorstep. My friends told me that they often fed him themselves, and in fact he was left to scrounge round and about – driven away from some doors, by the more primitive and ignorant types, taken in and given something by the more decent and kindly.

Enforcing my angry message, I left Chalky on his cold hearthstone and departed up the road. Again he did not at once track me, but within a remarkably short time he was up at the house again.

That evening his owner came up to reclaim him: a rather handsome young fellow, with modern hair-do on face – a masculine type. He took Chalky back on his shoulders: evidently familiar, but no intimate feeling on either side. I learned later that the little creature was now shut up for days, my only consolation being that at least he was safely off the roads.

I was looking forward greatly to seeing him when I came home in the spring. But, for a long time, he never appeared, perhaps because he was under the new régime.

Then one morning when the postman came, Chalky was suddenly there. He had come in with him, in his usual fashion, when the heavy black gate was opened. The postman was engaging me with some nonsense about his small girl having seen me on the visit I had paid to my old school, etc., when I caught sight of Chalky – in the familiar position at the entrance to the back-drive, diffident, asking whether he was welcome.

Welcome! I paid no further attention to the postman, dropped him in the middle of his sentence with 'There he is!' – to the man's surprise.

This time there was no doubt that Chalky had not forgotten me. He sprang into my arms and up on to my shoulders. I carried him indoors, set him down in the hall – where, looking round for me, he made for the kitchen.

This time he was unmistakably hungry. Fortunately there was something good going, and Beryl gave him a good meal of meat-scraps. That over, I brought his bowl of milk into the library where I was working.

I fetched the green velvet stool, which Peter – too apt to claw it with pleasure – was not allowed to sit on, spread the many-coloured woollen scarf Beryl had knitted for me, and drew it up to the desk beside me. Without a motion he knew it was for him and, before he had finished his milk, leaped up beside me.

It was evident that he wanted love as much as food. He once tried moving nearer, from his stool on to my lap, but found that there really wasn't room between me and the writing-table. Once he jumped down to finish his milk, but immediately came back without a word – no need to coax him, as with Peter.

He just knew. Strange, as Joan said, that with such a life he had such beautiful, engaging manners. Yes, that was the word for him – above all things, *engaging*: gay, courageous, having to fend for himself, yet wanting love more than anything. Joan observed that he can have had no sense of security whatever – brought up to be loved by the little girl, then neglected. He was a perfect cat, with such good manners and responsiveness, in spite of the treatment he had received. I think of Hardy's phrase, with tears: 'Who thinketh no ill'.

For that morning the little cat found security. Fed and contented, he was tired and sleepy – he must have been scrambling round all night. He lay there quite quiet, with the tiniest, hardly audible purr, occasionally looking up to see if I was there. I worked away, happy to have his company, at my book on Westminster Abbey, for Ambassador Walter Annenberg.

Once, when I had to leave the room to get a book, Chalky lifted himself up, concern in his eyes. I raised an admonitory

finger and told him that I'd be back. He sank down re-
assured and fell into deep sleep. Thus we spent a happy
morning: I at work, my little companion beside me; he in
contentment and security.

But only for that morning. There came my lunch-time and
after-lunch rest. And Beryl: 'He's not to stay up here in the
house. He has his own home: he must go down there. It isn't
fair,' etc. Though I well understand the motive behind these
representations, perhaps, after all, it *wasn't* fair.

Weakly, regretfully, I put him outside the library window
to make his way home. It was the last time I ever saw him.

Caught in a dilemma, I had planned a clever compromise.
Since I couldn't take him on, in spite of his adopting *me*,
I would leave things as they were. His unsatisfactory home
could keep him in term-time when I was away, while I would
have him up with me when at home in the vacations. It
would be a very convenient arrangement.

From Oxford I always used to telephone to Peter on Mon-
days at six. Beryl would hold him up to the receiver and,
when he recognised my voice, he would purr loudly all the
way to Oxford.

When I inquired for Chalky, Beryl hadn't seen him, either
up at the house or down in the village. Weeks passed, and
he was missing from his home. No-one had seen or heard of
him. No-one has heard a word of him since.

And I am miserable about him. I failed him just like everybody else. I was no better about him than anybody else –
worse, for I designed to have his love on the cheap. And he
had chosen me, expressed his confidence in me. Which I
betrayed, just like everybody else. So much worse, for I at
least understood the situation in all its bearings.

And in some strange way it links up with the mystery of
life – the mysterious inevitability of things, the irrevoc-
ability of what happens, the implacable sentence that time
passes. If only one could reverse it, if only one could have

one's chance over again! This little affair, my brief acquaintance with this young cat that never belonged to me, that gave me his confidence, which I betrayed, that could have been mine had I been willing to take the trouble to take him on – it is all an image of the crux at the heart of things: love offered and denied, the judgment from which there is no appeal.

I at any rate have paid the penalty for my betrayal with an aching heart and many tears. But what is the good of that? It won't bring him back. Nothing will ever bring him back.

Wherever I look around here, especially in those few places associated with him, I see his image still: most of all, by the upper gate where he used to come in from the road, pausing with back to the hedge to ask if he was welcome; or outside the gate at the bottom of the garden, where I left him looking back, with mute reproach, in the lane; or scampering along the hall, turning to make sure I was there and slipping up on the polished floor; inside my bedroom door daintily cleaning himself for the night; or here, asleep and contented, at last secure, on the green velvet stool beside me in the library where I write this now alone. The perfect friend and companion, cheerful and courageous, above all, with a way of endearing himself: a brave little spirit, confronting the chances of life just like the rest of us. In his case, alone. Nothing can console me for my failing him, or to think that I shall never see him again – never, never, never.

PART THREE

Tommer, the Black Farm-Cat

CHAPTER ONE
'Little Black Mug'

I have often been asked, by people who have read *Peter, the White Cat of Trenarren*, if he had a successor. I thought I had made it clear that, like Thomas Hardy, I couldn't bear to take on a cat full-time again, love him as I did Peter and then have my heart rent when he died.

One lady in B B C Television told me that my little book about Peter helped her when she was distraught by the death of her favourite cat. She lay in wait for me, on a visit I was paying to the South Bank T V complex, to tell me how miserable she had been. It is touching to think of the confidence and love that can subsist between the animals and us. Well, we are – or were once – animals ourselves: I shall have something more philosophic to say about that later.

Meanwhile, I am struck, somewhat surprised, and always moved, by the touching confidence these little creatures display in us – when some humans are simply odious in their treatment of them. And yet I have known *them* continue to love when beaten and ill-treated. I cannot bear that, or even to think of it. (And it adds to my queasy feeling about humans, my worst side – my liability to contempt for them. I never have any contempt for animals, poor creatures without our rational capacity and *therefore* obligations.)

The little fellow that infiltrated his way into my life unsought, and unexpectedly, was a wild farm-cat from the farm in the valley below the house. I had long known him, without taking particular notice of him. He was a small black tomcat, who would never come near one. The only times I saw him were when he sometimes crossed the paddock – former flower-garden – when I happened to be working there. I would speak to him, hold out a friendly hand, but he would never stop, just ran on keeping a safe distance.

So I was never much interested in him, though I had this acquaintance with him over years. He must have known Peter – without being friends. Peter was neutered, and rather a pansy; the little black cat was complete, and a bit of a ranger, quite undomesticated. He lived out of doors, and slept with the other animals in the barn below.

Came a day when the farmer died, and his widow was ill in hospital. Their son, farming some distance away, came once a day to put down some food for the dog, Spot, and the cats. I suspect that the dog got the lion's share, and this meant a crisis for them all.

Day after day Spot and two or three cats would come up to our back door hopefully for food. Phyllis's theory was that she didn't like animals, and was positively afraid of dogs. We were not going to take on the responsibility of feeding other people's animals. However, we had to do something: we saved up bones and scraps. My gardener-friend, Jack, who had been so good to Peter in all my absences in America, brought down a bagful of scraps twice a week.

It wasn't enough. Every morning there would be the faithful company waiting patiently at the door. So I took it into my head to go over to Monte Carlo – as we call the old mining village of Mount Charles (after Charles Rashleigh who built the original miners' cottages) – to lay in a stock of dog-biscuits.

Spot liked them and came to expect them; the cats got used to them in the end.

We soon noticed, however, that when the food was thrown out, the little black cat missed out: he got hardly anything, he was so slow, the others so quick. We thought he was stupid – and, the most impatient of men, I can't stand a stupid slow-coach.

We knew that he was old, and at last we noticed – we were slow in the uptake – that he couldn't see very well. So that was why he always got left out.

90

It took me a little time to realise that he was feeble and ill. He was not at all attractive to look at: one eye was perpetually running, his face puffed, so that I called him 'Little Black Mug'. A great contrast to the so much loved Peter, handsome white Persian.

Once I spotted the poor little black mug's condition, I took special measures.

He didn't seem to have any teeth to crack up the dog biscuits, as the other cats could. He was having no nourishment, so frail and ill he just couldn't compete with the others – though every morning he was there. How he dragged himself up from the farm I don't know.

So I got in the way of taking out a little hammer to crack up his dog-biscuit on the big granite step. And, next thing, I gave him a little milk. Not much, for he was so famished that I noticed that he could take very little, and he occasionally brought up again the milk or milk sops we gave him.

He still remained outside the door with the others, but was beginning to be protected and looked after. So he remained on in the back court when the others had gone – formed the habit of staying up here most of the day, though he still went home for the night, down the steep lawn, across the paddock and along the farm lane to the barn.

I had no intention of adopting him, to take the place of Peter: he was a farm-cat, not house-trained, not used to indoor life. I was not particularly taken with him, and did not attempt to pick him up. He wouldn't have allowed that anyway. He was independent and self-contained, with a will of his own, but weak and old and ill.

Phyllis wondered whether he had any teeth left; I never dared to look, he would not have let me get near him. He was not like Peter, who, when ill, would allow me to open his mouth, pop the vet's pill in, and hold his jaws until he had swallowed it. He was a most obedient cat.

We learned the little tomcat's name: not Tom, nor Tommy, but (Cornish) Tommer.

In summer-time Phyllis and I would take our coffee out for elevens, or tea at tea-time, on the terrace, looking down the lawn bordered by rhododendrons, camellias, hydrangeas, to the valley beyond and the small hamlet of Trenarren to the blue sea of the bay.

After some time, Tommer would come round the corner from the back court to join us. He seemed to like company, though still not permitting the liberty of even touching him. Next thing, I installed his own little glass dish by our seat on the terrace, so that he could have his elevens – milk, never too much – too.

He came to appreciate this attention. The only way he would show it, for he was still weak, was to roll over on his side once in the sun, and then roll back again. Still keeping his distance from us. I once put a hand out to touch his flank; his response was a little hiss of displeasure and he extended a claw. Actually his claws seemed to be permanently extended, fixed I suppose with old age; but they still could scratch. He made hardly more than the gesture.

He was still too weak to purr – if he knew how to. His eye was still running. A little later, when he had gained more confidence with me I tried to attend to it, wipe it gently with cotton wool. Not with much success; it was evidently still painful, both eyes puffed from starvation. Not a pretty cat – still just Little Black Mug.

The treatment continued – on his own terms. Not that I thought of it as treatment: I didn't know whether we should save the life of the poor little fellow. He wasn't our cat; I had no intention of adopting him, like Peter who had shared my home, lived with us, often gone to bed with me.

All cats are routineers; and this little tom soon got into the regular routine. He recognised the hammer in my hand as for him, accompanying his ration of biscuit – when Spot flinched away from the sight (evidently he knew what it was to receive a blow). Tommer had no fear, fitted into the pattern of being favoured, specially treated; and recognised the glass dish by the bench on the terrace as his own.

I can't remember the stages by which he got stronger and better; I think he owed his recovery more to Phyllis than to me. In spite of her protestations she was kind to him; and fed him more than I did.

Besides, I had to be away – last year on a visit to America to lecture at the Metropolitan (Museum, not Opera!), on 'Shakespeare and the Arts'. Thence up into New England to Miss Porter's famous school at Farmington, Connecticut – where I haven't forgotten the large and splendid cat, very much at ease in Zion, who came out and confidently displayed his friendliness, walking amid all the arriving cars.

When I got home I was a little surprised, and not a little pleased, that Tommer had not forgotten me – had perhaps missed me, for he gave me a welcome and was undeniably more forthcoming.

And he was better. His eye had recovered, though his sight was not good on that side; his face was no longer puffed – he was no longer Little Black Mug. And he had developed an appetite, was no longer so weak, or ill. He was old – so old: the farmer's wife, herself recovered and returned, told us that he must be nearing twenty.

He was still thin and a bit scraggy. His coat around neck and shoulders had recovered a nice black sheen; the rest of him was rusty coloured. But he was no longer unattractive: he was a nice little tomcat.

There was further evidence of Tommer's recovery. He absented himself for three days down in the orchard, as I surmised.

Peter, having been doctored, did not know the 'facts of life'. Like his master – or, rather friend (who had been three times doctored) – he found them distasteful.

Not so Tommer. A stray female had been around the place

displaying her charms, and at last, tempted, he went off to do his duty.

And came back, after some three days, rather the worse for wear. I regarded him with an unfavourable, perhaps a jaundiced, eye. But I refrained from behaving badly, remembering D.H.Lawrence who beat his bitch when she deserted him to go with a dog, and returned crestfallen. Lawrence had an acute intuitive sense with animals, and was certain that his bitch understood his reaction at her desertion – though there was more to it than that.

I am persuaded that the females of the species are more clever than the males, and that she-cats are cleverer than tomcats. Tommer was slow in the uptake and rather stupid; Peter had not been a clever cat. I did not love him the less for that, perhaps rather the more (contrariwise with humans – stupid ones I cannot abide, when our mental capacities are all we have to distinguish us from the animals).

So Master (the phrase is a mark of disapprobation) Tommer, after a few days' coolness at his fall from grace and his retrograde state, was reinstated. Did he too understand? He never slunk away again.

He now became more forthcoming and made advances. He would not only allow me to touch him and stroke his head – not his body, let alone tickle his belly (which Peter had loved) – but at elevenses on the terrace, when Phyllis and I were drinking our coffee and he had finished his milk, he would crawl up my leg and try sitting in my lap.

I don't think he had ever been taken up and fondled, for he didn't care for sitting in my lap; he preferred to go on up my arm until he was comfortably lying across my shoulder. This became his favourite position, and of course I conformed. With cats you have to do what *they* like: you can't inflict on them what *you* like, as with dogs. There is one difference.

By this time he knew that he was favoured; the other ani-

mals knew it too, and accepted it. Tommer was old and –
like a Fellow of an Oxford college – enjoyed the privileges
(and disadvantages) of seniority. The others still came up
regularly every morning, though the farmer's widow had
returned. After being fed they usually went away; Tommer
remained all day. He found it more interesting up here.

As long as he lived the others came regularly. Phyllis said
that he 'slocked' them (Cornish for 'enticed' or 'attracted');
he certainly was the centre of attraction for me. He had his
own little personality, a decided individuality. The others
took second place. There were the dog Spot; a beautiful
young tortoise-shell she-cat, Tiger; and a curious stray cat,
glossy black with white waistcoat, like a waiter, who had
the name Flip.

I used to call them my little family. First thing, when I
came down in the mornings, I would ask Phyllis: 'How is
the little family?'

CHAPTER TWO

The Little Family

Spot, as a dog, had different treatment from the cats. For one thing, being bigger, he had two biscuits or even three, where they had one each. For another, he always took his biscuit from my hand – oh, so gently, however hungry he was: he had been well trained, and had become a nice dog.

Earlier, when the farmer was alive and Spot was a working farm-dog, he was unapproachable by anybody but the family. He was an extremely nervous dog, highly strung and unreliable. The farmer used to warn me not to touch him – he would have snapped.

Not a large dog, mostly spaniel (I like all spaniels, not terriers, wiry and noisy), he was prettily marked: black spots well placed over white body, black ears with a touch of golden brown.

The love of his life had been his young mistress, who had deserted him – married and gone further up the valley to live, and brought a large sheep-dog to dominate the place. Spot wasn't wanted any longer – a miserable sensation for a man or an animal.

The life of the farm had come to an end, the family dispersed. Spot had been a working dog: how often have I seen him at the farmer's heel going out to round up the cattle, or coasting happily up the lane behind him, or returning from the day's work looking inquiringly, in no friendly fashion, at me.

Now there was nothing for him to do – and he undoubtedly grieved at being deserted. I don't understand much about dogs, but later – when I got to know him – I saw him sitting on our lawn, sniffing the air all round as if looking for someone he had lost, who yet was around, not far away.

By then I was on friendly terms and would put an arm

round to console him. He had become affectionate, but I was no real substitute for his lost love. Once I saw him when he met her in the lane – and it was the old pranks again, jumping up, paws against chest, tail whirling with excitement, barks of delirious happiness: he had found his youth again. But it was only a brief encounter.

Gradually he came to have confidence in me and to learn that a raised arm or a stick in hand didn't mean a blow. When I came back from a visit to America I was touched by his welcome after absence: he went round in circles on his own in front of me, not around me, giving little barks of joy. And the farmer's widow told Phyllis that, when he heard my voice down below, he would be off like a shot up here.

So I had at last won a place in his affections, though he was not demonstrative as he was with his mistress, with whom he had been young. Spot was now elderly and staid; I was old, if not staid – and he found me reliable and affectionate.

With animals it is not just all food: it is food *and* love and care of them. The first is a necessity, but they value the second even more: one can infer their scale of values for they mostly respond more to the second.

When Spot or the cats scuffled or snatched from each other, and Phyllis would say that one or the other was greedy, I would say, 'They have to eat, poor things, same as we have to.'

I never forget that men are animals, some of them just animals; some types you see slouching about the streets have evidently only recently descended from the trees.

It is thought that cats attached themselves to man and his habitats long before dogs did, making themselves useful domestically in catching rodents and vermin. They are much earlier in their domestication, and hence have remained more independent, can actually subsist, if not well, without man. Dogs, through man's intervention and centuries of breeding them, are much more man's creation and are dependent upon him.

Of course there are bad dogs, as there are bad humans. An Oxford friend of mine told me that his proletarian family in Staffordshire had a killer-dog. Not very big, he yet took pleasure in killing other dogs. He had a wicked way of mounting the wall and dropping from a height, to break the other animal's back. Nothing could stop him. He had to be 'put down' – as should be the case with humans of similar tendencies.

I hope it may be seen that my attitude towards animal creation is not based on sentimentalism – though of course sentiment enters in, and rightly.

I confess that there are even bad cats – actually killer-cats too. Michael Joseph in his best-seller about cats tells us of a horrid London prowler that would kill other cats. Why? He should have been put down, like humans who deliberately kill others. No sentiment comes into the matter, when others are not safe from them, the killers.

The only two bad cats I have known were both American, and both bullies. When charming Madeleine Doran, good Shakespeare scholar, came to research at the Huntington Library she took a house with a formidable cat next door. He would invade her premises for food and wouldn't go out; he would attack her if she tried to get him out. She had to resort to a broom to keep him at bay and push him out.

The other bad cat belonged to the Librarian of the Huntington, another large aggressive tom, who lived mostly out of doors and came in only for food. When the Librarian went on leave his house was taken for a time by my friend, the eminent Milton scholar, J.M.Steadman, who also took on looking after the cats (there were two). Instead of being grateful for being looked after, when it came to feeding time my friend had to keep a weather eye open or he would be attacked.

This must, however, be rare among cats, much more common among dogs.

I have known only one utterly unresponsive and uninteresting cat, a tabby who belonged to my dear old friend, Dr Stephens of Newquay, a philanthropic antiquarian and local doctor, to whom I dedicated *West Country Stories*. That cat never spoke to the doctor or his sisters, never purred or even growled, was utterly null. I tried all sorts of persuasions upon him which never fail with cats; he merely retreated under the table and sulked.

I have no use for that sort of cat – or person, for that matter.

Why do I like cats better than dogs, though fond of both? I am not one of those who can tolerate one, not the other. (Warden Sparrow of All Souls, for example, simply detests dogs.) It is true that they are more messy, more obvious and obstreperous, clumsy and apt to get in the way, to knock things over unnoticing. In that, they are like very masculine heterosexuals.

Cats have a feline, sinuous feminine grace and do not knock things over.

Rouben Mamoulian – creator of *Queen Christina* (Stalin's favourite film) and Greta Garbo's first great part – had the most beautiful cat I have ever seen, an Abyssinian, Abigail (about whom he wrote a book). In his exquisite pavilion-house in Beverly Hills I have seen Abigail wind her sinuous way over polished dinner-table, through a forest of knives and forks and spoons, glasses and dishes, plates and silver, not displacing or even touching an object.

Of course there are many more reasons why I prefer cats, some of a philosophic character. Cats, being more independent, are less demanding of attention, don't have to be taken for walks, etc., and are therefore more suitable writers' animals. Many are the writers, therefore, who have been devoted to them: Dr Johnson, Christopher Smart, the poet Gray and Horace Walpole, Matthew Arnold (who loved dogs too) and Théophile Gautier, who had forty cats – too many. I am in favour of monogamy where cats are concerned.

But the real reasons are simple and sensuous, more aesthetic. I prefer cats' fur to dogs' hair; I prefer the slightly aromatic, nutty smell of cats' fur; I don't like the *smell* of dogs. There is greater pleasure in stroking and smoothing feline fur, silky and soft. And they are much easier to pick up and carry about, sinuous and flexible, where dogs are bony and solid, heavier and difficult to put down. I adore the delicious sensation of a cat clinging to one, nestling into arms or hugging one's neck, purring the while – sometimes sizzling with sensuous pleasure themselves. They are more expressive, subtler, more complex and sensuous.

Dogs can't purr.

I suppose I must regard Tiger as the second member of the little family, always there in the mornings. A totally different personality from Tommer, a beautifully marked tortoise-shell: young and active, she could look after herself, a hunter.

She had the disadvantage of being a female, and I really couldn't have a family of kittens foisted on me – at rather frequent intervals too. (I had that chore years ago at Polmear, before coming to Trenarren with bachelor, indeed celibate, Peter.)

So I was discouraging and off-hand with beautiful Tiger – deliberately and rather regretfully. Not that she appeared to mind: a female, she was what the Cornish call 'forthy', ready to push forward and come indoors uninvited, unafraid. So unlike poor little Tommer, who waited to be asked.

Tiger was a pretty cat and very affectionate, lifted herself up on hind legs to be patted and stroked. I was sorry not to be kinder to her, for she too was thin, only half-fed. Unafraid, she would come up and take a biscuit from my hand like a dog. Tommer hadn't the sense for that: he would rub his head against my hand to make me drop his biscuit, and then there was the little hammer to break it up for him – which he recognised as his instrument.

The last member of the little family was a comic character, a black tomcat with white waistcoat, whose name I learned was Flip. A stray and a hunter, he seemed to be in good condition, not thin like the others. So I began by chasing him off. Occasionally I relented and threw him a biscuit out to the outer circle, for naturally he usually kept his distance.

Gradually he learned that my bark was worse than my bite, and, when really hungry, he would come to hand. Like Tommer, he didn't know how to take the biscuit, but would nuzzle my hand to drop it. Usually, however, he kept on the outer rim, but would answer to his name with a curious blink or two, and opening his mouth to answer. Together it made a comic face – a blinking cat.

Then, one day an incident happened which won my heart. All three cats were fond of Spot. Tommer had lived with him so many years that he took him for granted. The others gave him a welcome when he arrived, later in the mornings, fussing around him. Someone who had looked into the barn one evening saw Spot lying there, all three cats comfortably around him.

I noticed that Flip was particularly fond of the elderly dog, would walk all round him, tail erect with pleasure to see him, brushing his face, treading gently on his toes, purring to him no doubt.

But one day, looking out of the window, I saw a spectacle I had never witnessed before and should never have believed. Spot sat complacently there, with Flip sitting up on his haunches pawing Spot's chest, pounding away, rubbing and moulding his breast with both paws, while Spot maintained not merely composure but a look of sublime, fatuous complacency.

Evidently the young tomcat, a stray with no-one else to love, simply loved the dog. Have you ever known that, dear reader?

What a nice nature Flip must have! After that, I capitulated: he was welcome to the circle. He always remained nervous, aloof with me – naturally, after my chasing him off.

He couldn't be expected to understand that my chasing him was rather in inverted commas, not wholly serious.

There now arrived a fourth cat on the scene – the word had gone round. This was a very handsome outsider, a long-haired tabby tom, who evidently belonged to someone; for he was tame, well-fed and very much at ease in Zion.

Far too much so. Handsome and masculine he was very pleased with himself, and all too willing to enter the circle. He simply wouldn't take it from me that he wasn't wanted. He would sit there under the rhododendrons, or on the lawn, and not move when I gestured at him to go away. Phyllis and I thought that he must be a domestic cat, used to be somebody's pet. He was beautifully marked, in good condition, but looked back at one brazenly and with a very self-satisfied expression. He was like those people who won't even take 'Yes' for an answer. But he was not getting 'Yes' from me, for all his brazen persistence.

He took to keeping company there at the corner of the back-drive under the rhododendrons, a very cushy place in morning sun by the warm ferns, with Tiger, who had been Flip's friend. He was manœuvring Flip out.

One day Phyllis witnessed from her window a fight for who should be top cat. Locked in each other's embrace Flip and the new cat rolled from top to bottom of the bank – and the tabby emerged victor. There had already been a certain amount of caterwauling against each other, according to Phyllis – which I hadn't heard in the front of the house. She said it had kept her awake; I said that they were singing to her, giving her a concert.

But this was it: a male fight for mastery, like fatuous bulls in a herd fighting for top place with the cows.

The handsome tabby was victor, would stay in that corner by the ferns all night. When I took the morning tea along to Phyllis's room early, there he would be happily in the sun, waiting for Tiger. When she arrived they would be installed in their corner, a comfortable couple: the she-cat, in usual feminine manner having gone over to the conqueror, the tabby tom more brazen than ever, with a look of even more fatuous male complacency on his handsome features.

He had succeeded in driving Flip away. For days and days Flip didn't dare to come near the place. The powerful newcomer was in possession; Tiger, the she-cat, was his; this was his place.

He was much cleverer than Flip, let alone poor stupid old Tommer – who, favoured and protected, was well out of it. When I made a threatening gesture to the tabby to go away, he would retreat, but, immediately I had turned my back, would return. Master Impudence!

I entered upon a deliberate policy with him. Not very good at throwing stones, quite inaccurate in aim, I would regularly throw one in his direction. (Man's mastery of stone-throwing, the range his ape-like hand gave him, must have been his earliest aid in the struggle for survival.)

Though I never once hit the brazen tabby, consistent policy kept him at bay, on the outer circle. Gradually, furtively, nice Flip has taken to coming back, with the coast kept clear for him. Master Impudence is still about, trespassing in the background, but the message has at last got across his confident male egoism.

CHAPTER THREE
Love in Old Age

Tommer became transformed by the treatment he received. He had never known what it was to be loved before; he now discovered the delights of love in old age. And didn't he respond!

He became a perfectly sweet little cat. Phyllis and I – no sentimentalists – swore that we would not love him so much if he had not become so loving. And still I was determined not to adopt him, as he would have liked – after all, he did not belong to us – and I did not want to have my heart broken as after Peter's death. Tommer was already a good deal older than Peter was when he died.

Moreover, I liked the idea of ambivalence in cats, as in other matters. It is quite common for cats to have two homes, with lots of food. My friend Arthur Bryant had a celebrated cat, Sammy (though quite besotted with his Cornish dog, Jimmy – couldn't take a holiday abroad because Jimmy wouldn't like it, etc!). One day, having to get up very early in the morning, Arthur spied Sammy stealing out of his alternative home, where he had spent the night, to spend the day at Arthur's house in Rutland Gate.

Very well, let Tommer go home to spend the night with the others in the barn, get what he could of the morning ration and then come to spend the day up here. This was the routine that he henceforth followed most days.

He arrived up here very early, long before the others. I often look out of my bedroom window about dawn, or shortly after, it is so beautiful. The steep lawn, shelving down to the combe, still asleep, the trees hardly yet awake, though in the stillness one can hear them breathing, a faint rustle, like a sigh. In early summer there is the musky scent of the one scented rhododendron, or the honeyed fragrance of bluebells, thick on the bank. A little later comes the stronger smell from the lime-tree in flower; from the lawn the sharp tang of camomile amid the grass.

Most of all, I am held by the ice-blue colour of the bay through the trees to the east, pointing out towards the headland, beginning to be touched by the pale rose of dawn. Ice-blue and pale rose flush! I am held spellbound.

Then, in winter, by the time the morning tea is made and I go out into the corridor, the whole length of it and up the further stairs is aglow with the dawn coming in from the eastern staircase window. I have sometimes seen the light a rich mahogany colour, and – old as I am – it makes me thrill to be alive, alight with the beauty of the world:

> Look thy last on all things lovely
> Every hour . . .

It is a good gospel.

Very occasionally, thus early, I have seen Tommer making tracks from the farm up here. 'Making tracks' is the word for it; for, what with Spot and the cats, there was a track one could see distinctly in the dew, at the edge of the lawn all along the right hand flower-border. Still more marked on the rare occasion this winter when we had snow: a clear trackway from the path beside the huge rhododendron at the bottom – beyond that the steps, across the paddock, over the fence and into the farm-lane.

By the time I got round to Phyllis's room in the west wing Tommer would be waiting on the side door-step below; I would go down to let him in. If it was raining he would be sheltering right up against the door, oddly enough never very wet: cats' fur seems better protective covering than dogs' hair.

Tommer was not very keen on our milk. I sometimes wondered whether it wasn't too cold out of the fridge, and he would have been used to warm milk straight from the cows. He would lap water, just like Peter.

By the time elevenses came he had changed his mind, and a little procession was formed. I went ahead carrying him on my shoulder and a little jug of milk for him; Phyllis came behind with a cup of coffee in each hand for us. So we processed out of the side door, across the court and around the little library lawn to the terrace. We sometimes laughed, when caught thus by our friend Jack Gill, who wondered at the spectacle we should present on TV.

I don't think Tommer would have minded; he took no notice of having his photograph taken, whereas Peter hated it – it was dreadfully difficult to get a snap of him. He knew the camera (which I had specially bought to take pictures of him) and recognised the lens as the Evil Eye.

We seated ourselves on the seat outside my study window; once he had drunk his milk Tommer now would scramble up to his favourite place on my right shoulder.

The seat on the terrace became a favourite haunt. Thence he could keep an eye on me working away at the desk in front of the study window, occasionally peeping round to see if I was there. He liked it better still when I was working in the garden, in full view along the borders on each side of the lawn.

I had not noticed when he first developed this fixation on me. It was Phyllis who told me that – some time before I had fallen for him – when I was down in the paddock, below the big mountainous rhododendrons, a little sheltered world on its own (so close I don't much like working there), Tommer stayed there all afternoon perched on the branch of the rhodo for company. And I never even noticed him.

Phyllis and I agreed that he seemed to like our company better than that of the other animals. Perhaps it was a new experience for him, a discovery of human friendship made late in life. He liked our gardening friend, Jack, too – who had been kind to Peter over years. Regularly now Jack brought down scraps and tit-bits for the little family. They all knew him – and I would say Jack's name over and over to Tommer. He knew Phyllis's name from constant repetition. Like Peter, he had no name for me.

But there was no doubt about his fixation. Sometimes, on warm summer nights, he would spend the whole night on the seat below my bedroom window; and when I called his name would look up with a look of touching devotion. He never spoke; we never heard him mew; Phyllis thought that he had lost his voice.

There may have been something wrong with his throat. There is no doubt that he had been dreadfully ill, and wouldn't have survived if it had not been for our care of him. He was rewarding us with his silent look of love.

There was that look of utter devotion in his eyes, which my friend, the Oxford historian K.B.McFarlane, used to notice in his cat's eyes. Tommer did not even belong to me, but there it was. His bad eye had healed now, though it still looked a little odd; I am not sure how good he was at focusing – both cats and dogs seem uncertain and rely as much on smell. I point to their food with my finger demonstratively – an authoritarian finger – and they obediently follow, it would seem gratefully. Sometimes with a sharp command: 'There, silly!' Or, 'Eat it!'

No doubt whatever that Tommer loved being fussed over.

Several times he and Spot would come round together from their assembly in the side-court, outside the kitchen window, to look in on me at the study window in the front of the house. It was just as if they had said to each other, 'Let's go and see what *he*'s doing.'

But how do they say it?

We all know their obvious means of communication, their barks and growls, whines and squeaks of joy, mewing and caterwauling, hissing and purring.

But I have come to the conclusion that animals' subtler

means of communication is by telepathy. I confess that I arrived at this after reading the autobiography of an Oxford acquaintance, E. R. Dodds's *Missing Persons*.

There is no doubt whatever about the fact of telepathy and the common occurrence of telepathic experiences. Everybody knows them; almost everybody has had them. And it is not at all difficult to conceive of them in these days of wireless – similar phenomena.

The question is their status in our experience, their origin and significance, or possible use.

Some people would like to think that they suggest the possibility of communication with the dead. After a lifetime dedicated to psychical research – or such time as the Regius Professor of Greek could spare from Greek scholarship (*The Greeks and the Irrational*) – Dodds reached a total negative. And I agree with him.

Telepathy does not relate to any future state, but to our remote animal past. It was Freud who made the inspired suggestion, that telepathy was probably a mode of communication for us as animals before we developed speech, and that its survival – like some other phenomena in our experience as yet unaccounted for – is vestigial.

This view of the matter would account not only for the well known fact of telepathic communication between humans, but also for the known phenomena, quite familiar in fact, of telepathic communication between human beings and animals.

Again there is no doubt of the fact: here is the explanation.

There are well known stories of dogs that, when their master away at the war has been killed, have wilted and died.

I am pretty sure that Peter knew when I was returning home from Oxford or America. To be sure, there were rational evidences – my bedroom was being prepared, etc. – but his knowledge or expectation was pre-rational.

It does not appear to me to be difficult to conceive of that;

no more difficult to think of being on the same wavelength with an animal one loves and who returns one's love than with a human being.

Of course, as man has developed his rational faculty along with speech, the telepathic apparatus has become somewhat atrophied; and we all know that it is discontinuous, inconstant and quite unreliable with us now. (I have usually found it more in evidence when I have been off-colour or unwell.)

With the animals it is the phenomena of reasoning that are discontinuous, inconstant and unreliable – though the evidence suggests that dogs can put two and two together, and draw a conclusion.

Our faculty of speech exerts a fascination for all animals, birds too (I don't know about reptiles: the reptiles I know are all human). Cats and dogs cannot have enough of being talked to, sympathetically and affectionately: they will listen inexhaustibly, for ever. Many of them try to talk back – among cats, Siamese will especially. Though when it comes to mutual *talk*, I find it sad that we mostly cannot understand what they are trying to say.

Peter would answer me, with varying mews and cries, at varying pitch; but it was a limited vocabulary, and sometimes he seemed discouraged at my not understanding what he was saying. Tommer never spoke; he just looked and looked adoringly when I talked to him, and purred constantly from the moment I picked him up.

They have some alternatives, ways of attracting attention, warnings; dogs particularly will give warning of danger or strangers. Peter could do that, hearing the big entrance gate, when we did not – fur standing up with apprehension, arching his back, giving a little growl.

Only this morning Phyllis told me that Flip was trying to tell her something, came two or three times to attract her attention – until she found that Tiger had been shut in the outdoor lavatory.

An American lady, Penny Moyes, has written a book entitled *How to Talk to Your Cat*. But her cats were loquacious Siamese; conversation with Tommer was a one-way traffic.

When winter and bad weather approached, Phyllis installed a little box in the lobby, between side-door and kitchen, and made it comfortable with an old pillow. Hitherto, a favourite position was on the mat inside the door – draughty, I thought.

The question was whether he would take to the box, recognise what it was *for*. When I first put him plump in, out he immediately popped again – just like a cat. You can't *make* them do anything, impose anything on them, unlike a dog. They just have to do it at their own sweet will. And shortly we found Master Tommer comfortably installed – he had taken to it, tumbled to what it was for and that it was meant for him.

I must say he looked sweet and snug in his nest, as we called it. It was there that he responded most to being talked to. He would sit bolt upright while I talked endearments, and sometimes whispered them – he knew that this was special talk for him.

All animals like being told that they are beautiful, and recognise the word when constantly repeated and long drawn out: 'What a bew-ewtiful pussy cat you are', etc. He would draw himself up, preen himself, look very perky and proud. Truthfully, as I have said, he was not a beautiful cat, unlike Peter. His coat remained scraggy and rust-coloured; but, after he had recovered from his illness, with care and attention, head and shoulders became black and glossy. And now he submitted to being brushed, to the mesmerising tunes of 'Bew-ewtiful', or 'What a pooket-cattums', or, reciting in rhythm:

> What a bew-ewtiful pussy-dog,
> What a bewtiful cat.

Nonsense talk, as is well known, is the language of love; and he would purr contentedly back.

It is possible to hypnotise cats – the fearsome human eye – and I used to send Peter off to sleep that way. Tommer, entranced, would remain quite still. One gesture he received with complete confidence – it used to surprise me that neither he nor Peter showed the slightest fear at it – would be to run their muzzles into the hollow of my hand, like a trap, while I flicked their ears with my fingers.

Once I picked him up thus, carrying him into the kitchen where Phyllis and Jack were talking, with 'Isn't he bewtiful?' To which Phyllis replied, off-hand, 'Oh, 'ansome!', laughing at me. To this my response was, 'Oh, we mustn't hurt his little feelings.' It is a regular rule with me *never* to hurt an animal's feelings. I don't mind about humans: they can look after themselves. Phyllis held that she didn't care for animals; in fact, though not recognising it, she had fallen for Tommer and his pretty ways.

Nothing pushing or aggressive about him: he would peep inquiringly around the kitchen-door, where he wasn't supposed to enter. In her absence he would come in with me while I foraged among the tins – a noise he knew well – for one of her baked buns or cakes, which featured at tea-time.

Afternoon tea, in good weather, is often taken on the terrace. When he heard the rattle of teacups, or his name called, he would appear around the corner trotting eagerly with anticipation.

By late spring the familiar chaffinches and bluetits would be back from wherever they went for winter (Morocco?). It always amazes me that these little creatures know their way back across hundreds, or a thousand, miles to the accustomed spot. How?

There they would be, the winter over, up in the familiar magnolia, eyeing the tea-table with bright eyes, waiting for crumbs. And extraordinarily tame. They would approach quite near; sometimes, when hungry in nesting-time would flutter exquisitely beside the garden-table, pick up a piece of bread and hurry off with it down the lawn or across to a nest among the rhododendrons. I have known one of them – the hen-birds tamer or braver than the males – perch on the arm of the seat beside me.

Tommer, having had his tea, would be lying on the gravel, eyeing the small bird as she came fearlessly nearer, almost within range. Sometimes I would become alarmed and throw a scrap of food further away; but Tommer never made the slightest gesture towards them, or even showed much interest. Too old, I suppose. The tiny birds, for their part, knew him quite well and took him for granted, a regular feature of the tea-time scene.

A robin, I noticed, was more careful to keep his distance. The tiny bluetits appear the friendliest and most tamable of birds. They have an exquisite way of scurrying and scrambling delicately up and down the japonica outside my study-window. They recognise me when I come out to seat myself at the garden-table; sometimes we have had as many as four or five of them flitting and flipping about, coloured wings blue, green, grey fluttering against magnolia, japonica, grey gravel, green lawn, blue sea.

Oh, I forgot to say that Tommer, though not beautiful, now had – in my opinion – a sweet little face, eyes a bit irregular (after his long illness) and the usual pretty nose of a cat.

Inside the house his home was the lobby at the side door. He didn't like upstairs at all. I suppose he had never been upstairs. Once or twice he allowed me to carry him up those unintelligible stairs – dangerous, if you fell, so he held on tight – to pay Phyllis a visit in bed in the early morning. But that was out of his experience, and it was not welcomed; he was glad to be back safe on the ground-floor again. And once, when Phyllis brought him up to see me in bed, he positively objected: he hardly recognised me, he was so fussed – not natural to see me in such a place.

He was choosy, too, about the downstairs rooms. He didn't like the study, a favourite haunt of Peter's, who spent many hours on my lap in the big armchair. In that room he would listen to me telephoning to him from Oxford.

Tommer didn't know the dining-room, though he would sometimes take a scrap from my hand at the window. (Spot more often.) Tommer liked the library best. When the big Georgian window was open at the bottom he could infiltrate and go to sleep in one of the red-and-white stripey armchairs I had brought down from my rooms at Oxford.

When I was working at the table, he would try the purple velvet armchair nearest to where I was working. I would put a cushion on it so that he did not scratch the velvet. Then he would climb up over the arm to get nearer, what he really wanted, of course, was to get up on my shoulder.

I couldn't have that, writing away as I was at prefaces to Shakespeare's plays or copying out longhand the Dark Lady's poems to all the countesses she knew – or didn't know.

Sometimes, when he was insistent on climbing up over the arm, I would compromise and try writing with him on my lap. But there wasn't room for him and he would jump down to wander restlessly around the room. I was really rather relieved when he went to the door to be let into the lobby, his little nest, and the promising smells from the kitchen.

Then I could concentrate and get on with my work.

There followed an episode which worried us greatly – which shows that he had woven his way into our hearts: he was missing for a couple of days. We wondered if he was ill again. We telephoned to the farmer's widow: no, she had not seen him, he had not been down in the barn with the rest.

Where could he be?

At last, after two days, Phyllis noticed sheerly by accident that somehow he had got through – or fallen through – the grating that allows light to the windows of the cellars on the side of the court.

He hadn't got into the cellar, for the window was closed. There the poor little fellow was stuck, with no voice to give a mew and tell us where he was – and he couldn't get back up from that depth. Down we hurried, knocked open a pane of the fixed window and out he came – not apparently the worse for wear, though dreadfully thirsty after a couple of days without food or drink.

What Tommer wanted, evidently, was to share my life, as Peter had done. He was constantly trying to infiltrate into the house. But, in the first place, he didn't belong to us; and again, unlike Peter, he wasn't house-trained.

Several times, in bad weather, we let him stay in his nest in the lobby all night – but there was usually an accident. We installed a cat-tray full of cinders by the door, and he did seem to tumble to what that was for, though we didn't like this installation.

I fear the real reason was cowardice on my part: I didn't want to be so dreadfully upset, when the end came, as I was over Peter. Tommer was already older – we never knew exactly how old. I was in favour of his having two homes – at least of his going down at night to the barn and the company of the other animals.

It really appeared that he preferred our company, which he had discovered so late in life.

He was on his last legs; we accepted that he would not be with us much longer. We had recovered him from his famishing illness, so that he had had a good last two years of life, more interesting and varied than anything he had known before.

There were those endearments he had come to know and welcome – rubbing noses, as all cats like (dogs not: with them, their tongues are extraordinarily sensitive and flexible). He had not been accustomed to being kissed on his little head, and would crouch down coyly, pretending not to like it, while purring loudly the while. He came to recognise this as an endearment.

At the end, like Peter, he ceased to be able to eat. There in the mornings he still would be, waiting for the sound of the bolts being drawn. I would put down the best cream off the top of the milk; he took a few laps at it but could take no more.

On his last night he really did not want to go home, to his original home. We repented sadly that we sent him out as usual, into the night – and never saw him again.

We tried to console ourselves with the thought that we had made those last two years for him. All the same, we missed him sorely those first days and weeks; and, though I had been determined not to be upset, I wept for him.

He *had* wound his way into our hearts with his pretty little ways. Every morning when I go into Phyllis's room with her tea, I think of him as I look down into the court: no Tommer there on the doorstep early, waiting to come in.

We miss him again when coming back to the house in the car. I would give a couple of toots to let him know that we were back. He would have spent the afternoon sleeping on his favourite seat on the terrace, and now come peeping round the corner with an eager welcome.

How we miss his little black mug, dear Tommer, dear little soul!